The Way of Illumination and Cosmic Consciousness

The Man-God Whom We Await; The Lives of Prophetic and Spiritual Figures, Ancient and Modern

By Ali Nomad

Pseudonym of Alexander McIvor-Tyndall

Published by Pantianos Classics

ISBN-13: 978-1717119162

First published in 1913

Contents

The Self and Symbol iv

Argument v

Chapter One - The New Birth: What It Is: Instances Described 11

Chapter Two - Man's Relation to God and to His Fellow-Men ... 21

Chapter Three - Areas of Consciousness 30

Chapter Four - Self-Ness and Selflessness 38

Chapter Five - Instances of Illumination and Its Effects 46

Chapter Six - Examples of Cosmic Consciousness, Who Have Founded New Systems of Religion 54

Chapter Seven - Moses, The Law-Giver 61

Chapter Eight - Gautama—The Compassionate 64

Chapter Nine - Jesus of Nazareth 69

Chapter Ten - Paul of Tarsus 76

Chapter Eleven – Mohammed 84

Chapter Twelve - Emanuel Swedenborg 92

Chapter Thirteen - Modern Examples of Intellectual Cosmic Consciousness: Emerson; Tolstoi; Balzac 96

Chapter Fourteen - Illumination as Expressed in the Poetical Temperament 108

Chapter Fifteen - Methods of Attainment: The Way of Illumination 121

The Self and Symbol

Thou most Divine! above all women
Above all men in consciousness.
Thou in thy nearness to me
Hast shown me paths of love.
Yea; walks that lead from hell
To the great light; where life and love
  Do ever reign.
Thou hast taught to me a patience
To behold whatever state;
However beautiful and joyful; however ugly and sorrowful.
To know that these are—all!—but
The glimmerings of the greater life—
Expressions of the infinite.
According to the finality of that moment
Now to come; in the eternal now, which thou
Sweet Presence, hast awakened me to—
I see the light—the way.
An everlasting illumination
That takes me to the gate; the open door
To the house of God.
There I find most priceless jewels;
The key to all the ways,
That lead from Om to thee.
A mistake—an off-turn from the apparent road of right
Is but the bruising of thy temple,
Calling thy Self—thy soul—
The God within; showing thee,
The nita of it all; which is but the half of me.
And as thy consciousness of the two
The nita and the ita, comes to thee
A three is formed—the trinity is found.
Through thee the Deity hast spoken
Uniting the two in the one;
Revealing the illusion of mortality
The message of Om to the Illumined.

—Ali Nomad.

Argument

Man is essentially a spiritual being.

The source of this spiritual Omniscience we may not, in our finite intelligence, fully cognize, because full cognition would preclude the possibility of finite expression.

The destiny of man is perfection.

Man perfected becomes a god.

"Only the gods are immortal," we are told.

Let us consider what this means, supposing it to be an axiom of truth.

Mortality is subject to change and death. Mortality is the manifest—the stage upon which "man in his life plays many parts."

Immortality, is what the word says it is—godhood re-cognized in the mortal. "Im" or, "Om"—the more general term—stands for the Changeless. Birthless. Deathless. Unnamable Power that holds the worlds in space, and puts intelligence into man.

Biologists, even though they were to succeed in reproducing life by chemical processes from so-called "lifeless" (sterilized) matter, making so high a form of manifestation as man himself, yet could never name the power by which they accomplished it.

Always there must remain the Unknowable—the Absolute.

"Om," therefore, is the word we use to express this Omniscient, Omnipotent and Omnipresent power.

The term "mortal" we have already defined. The compound immortal, applied to individual man, stands for one who has made his "at-one-ment" with Om, and who has, while still in the mortal body, re-cognized himself as one with Om.

This is what it means to escape the "second death," to which the merely mortal consciousness is subject.

This is the goal of every human life; this is the essence, the substance of all religious systems and all philosophies.

The only chance for disputation among theologians and philosophers, lies in the way of accomplishing this at-one-ment. There is not the slightest opportunity for a difference of opinion as what they wish to accomplish.

Admitting then, that the goal of every soul is the same—immortality—(the mortal consciousness cognizing itself as Om), we come to a consideration of the evidence we may find in support of this axiom. This evidence we do not find satisfactory, in spirit communication; in psychic experiences; in hypnotic phenomena; and astral trips; important, and reliable as these many psychic research phenomena are.

These are not satisfactory or convincing evidences of our at-one-ment with Om, because they do not preclude the probability of the "second death;" but on the contrary, they verify it.

However, aside from all these psychic phenomena, there is a phase of human experience, much more rare but becoming somewhat general, that transcends phenomena of every kind.

The western world has given to these experiences the term "cosmic consciousness," which term is self explanatory.

The Orientals have long known of this goal of the soul, and they have terms to express this, varying with the many types of the Oriental mind, but all meaning the same thing. This meaning, from our Occidental viewpoint, is best translated in the term liberation, signifying to be set free from the limitations of sense, and of self-consciousness, and to have glimpsed the larger area of consciousness, that takes in the very cosmos.

This experience is accompanied by a great light, whether this light is manifested as spiritual, or as intellectual power, determines its expression.

The object of this book is to call attention to some of the more pronounced instances of this Illumination, and to classify them, according as they have been expressed through religions enthusiasm; poetical fervor; or great intellectual power.

But we have also one other argument to make, and this we present with a conviction of its truth, while conceding that it must remain a theory, until proven, each individual, man or woman, for himself and herself. The postulate is this: immortality (i.e. godhood) is bi-sexual. No male person can by any possibility become an immortal god, in, of and by himself; no female person can be complete without the "other half" that makes the ONE.

Each and every SOUL, therefore, has its spiritual counterpart—its "other half," with which it unites on the spiritual plane, when the time comes for attainment of immortality.

Sex is an eternal verity. The entire Cosmos is bi-sexual. Everything in the visible universe; in the manifest, is the result of this universal principle. "As above so below," is a safe rule, as far as the IDEA goes. This hypothesis does not preclude perfection above, of that which we find below, but any radical reversion or repudiation of nature is inconceivable.

"Male and female created he them." This being true, male and female must they return to the source from which they sprung, completing the circle, and gaining what?

Consciousness of godhood; of completeness in counterpartal union. Not absorption of consciousness, but union, which is quite a different idea.

Out of this counterpartal union a race of gods will be born, and these supermen, shall "inherit the earth" making it a "fit dwelling place for the gods."

This earth is now being made fit. This fact may seem a far distant hope if we do not judge with the eyes of the seer, but its proof lies in the emancipation of woman. Its evidences are many and varied, but the awakening of woman is the cause.

This awakening of woman constitutes the first rays of the dawn—that long-looked for Millenium, which many of us have regarded as a mere figure of speech, instead of as a literal truth.

The argument is not that there has been no individual awakening until the present time; but that never before in the finite history of the world has there been such a general awakening, and as it is self evident that conditions will reflect the idea of the majority, the fact that woman is being given her rightful place in the sense-conscious life, proves that the earth will be a fit dwelling place for a higher order of beings than have hitherto constituted the majority.

The numerous instances of Illumination, or cosmic consciousness which are forcing attention at the present time, prove that there is a race-awakening to a realization of our unity with Om.

Another point which we trust these pages will make clear is this: So-called "revelation" is neither a personal "discovery," nor any special act of a divine power. "God spake thus and so to me," is a phrase which the self-conscious initiate employs, because he has lost sight of the cosmic light, or because he finds it expedient to use that phraseology in delivering the message of cosmic consciousness.

If we will substitute the term "initiation," for the term "revelation," we will have a clearer idea of the truth.

Perhaps some of our readers will feel that the terms mean the same, but for the most part, those who have employed the word "revelation," have used it as implying that the plan of the cosmos was unfinished, and that the Creator, having found some person suitable to convey the latest decision to mankind, natural laws had been suspended and the revelation made.

It is to correct this view, that we emphasize the distinction between the two words.

The cosmos is complete. "As it was in the beginning, it is now and ever shall be, worlds without end."

A circle is without beginning or end. We, in our individual consciousness may traverse this circle, but our failure to realize its completeness does not change the fact that it is finished.

We can not add to the universal consciousness; nor take away therefrom.

But we can extend our own area of consciousness from the narrow limits of the personal self, into the heights and depths of the atman and who shall set limitations to the power of the atman, the higher Self, when it has attained at-one-ment with Om?

It is not the purpose of this book to trace the spiritual ascent of man further than to point out the wide gulf between the degrees of consciousness manifested in the lower animals and that of human consciousness; again tracing in the human, the ever-widening area of his cognition of the personal self, and its needs, to the awakening of the soul and its needs; which needs include the welfare of all living things as an absolute necessity to individual happiness.

Altruism, therefore, is not a virtue. It is a means of self-preservation—without this degree of initiation into the boundless area of universal, or cosmic consciousness, we may not escape the karmic law.

The revelations, therefore, upon which are founded the numerous religious systems, are comparable with the many and various degrees of initiation into THAT WHICH IS.

They represent the degree which the initiate has taken in the lodge.

It may be argued that this fact of individual initiation into the ever-present truth of Being, as into a lodge, offers no proof that this earth is to ultimately become a heaven. It may be that this planet is the outer-most lodge room and that there will never be a sufficient number of initiates to make the earth a fit dwelling place for a higher order of beings than now inhabit it. This may, indeed, be true. But all evidence tends toward the hope that even the planet itself will come under the regenerating power of Illumination.

All prophecies embody this promise; all that we know of what materialists call "evolution" and occultists might well name "uncovering of consciousness," points to a time when "God's will," "shall be done on earth as it is in heaven."

All who have attained to cosmic consciousness in whatever degree, have prophecied a time, when this blessing would descend upon every one; but the difficulty in adequately explaining this great gift seems also to have been the burden of their cry.

Jesus sought repeatedly to describe to his hearers the wonders of the cosmic sense, but realized that he was too far in advance of the cyclic end; but even as at that time, a number of disciples were capable of receiving the Illumination, so to-day, a larger number are capable of attainment. If this number is great enough to bring about the regeneration—the perfecting—of the earth conditions, then it must be accomplished.

We believe that it is. We make the claim that the Millenium has dawned; and although it may be many years before the light of the morning breaks into the full light of the day, yet the rays of the dawn are dispelling the world's long night.

In his powerful and prophetic story "In the Days of the Comet," H.G. Wells, tells of a great change that comes over the world following an atmospheric phenomenon in which a "green vapor" is generated in the clouds and falls upon the earth with instantaneous effect.

As this peculiar vapor descends, it has the effect of putting every one to sleep; this sleep continues for three days and when people finally awake, their interior nature has undergone a complete change.

Where before they "saw dimly," they now see clearly; the petty differences and quarrels are perceived in their true perspective. Instead of place, and power, and influence, and wealth, being all-important goals of ambition as before the change, every one now strives to be of service to the world. Love and kindness become greater factors than commercial expediency and business success.

In many respects, Wells' description of the great change and its effect upon people, corresponds with the effect of Illumination.

The sense of entering into the very heart of things; of growing plants; the birds and the little wood animals; the intense sympathy and understanding of life described by him, sounds like the effect of cosmic consciousness, as related by nearly all who have attained it.

How the world's activities are resumed after the change, and under what vastly different incentives people work, form a part of the story, which is written as fiction, but which contains the seed of a great truth.

This truth is expressed in science, as human achievement, and in religion as fulfilled prophecy, but the truth is the same.

Both religion and science point to a time when this earth will know freedom from strife and suffering. Even the elements which have hitherto been regarded as beyond the boundaries of man's will, may be completely controlled; not may be, but will be. Manual labor will cease. National Eugenic societies will put a stop to war, when they come to the inevitable conclusion, that no race can by any possibility be improved, while the most perfect physical species are reserved for armies.

Awakening woman will refuse—indeed they are now refusing—to bear children to be shot down in warfare, and crushed under the juggernaut of commercial competition.

Those who realize the signs of the times, look for the birth of cosmic consciousness as a race-consciousness, foreshadowing the new day; the "second coming of Christ," not as a personal, vicarious sacrifice, but as a factor in human attainment.

"For I am persuaded," said St. Paul, "that neither death nor life, nor angels, nor principalities, nor things present, nor things to come, nor powers, nor height, nor depth, nor any other creature shall be able to separate us from the love of God."

If we interpret this in the light of cosmic consciousness, we realize that we shall know, and experience that boundless, deathless, perfect, satisfying, complete and all-embracing love which is the goal of immortality; which is an attribute (we may say the one attribute) of God.

We are not looking for the birth of a Christ-child, but of the Christ-child; we are not looking for a second coming of a man who shall be as Jesus was, but we are anticipating the coming of the man (homo), who shall be cosmically conscious, even as was Jesus of Nazareth; as was Guatama, the Buddha.

That there may be one man and one woman who shall first achieve this consciousness and realization is barely possible, but the preponderance of evidence is for a more general awakening to the light of Illumination.

"We shall not all sleep, but we shall all be changed in the twinkling of an eye," said St. Paul.

The prophecy of "the woman clothed with the sun, and with the moon under her feet," is not of a woman, but of Woman, in the light of a race of men who have attained cosmic consciousness.

Nothing more is needed to make a heaven of earth, than that the great light and love that comes of Illumination, shall become dominant.

It will solve all problems, because problems arise only because we are groping in the dark. The elimination of selfishness; of condemnation; of fear and anger, and doubt, must have far greater power for universal happiness and well-being than all the systems which theology or science or politics could devise. Indeed, all these systems are sporadic and empirical attempts to express the vague dawning of Illumination.

In the fullness of its light, the need for systems will have passed away.

Chapter One - The New Birth: What It Is: Instances Described

The chief difference between the religions and the philosophies of the Orient and those of the Occident, lies in the fact that the Oriental systems, methods, and practices, emphasize the assumption that the goal of these efforts, is attainable at any moment, as it were.

That is, Oriental religion—speaking in the broad sense—teaches that the disciple need not wait for the experience called death to liberate the Self, the atman, from the enchantment or delusion, the maya, of the external world. Indeed, the Oriental devotee well knows that physical death, mrityu, is not a guarantee of liberation; does not necessarily bring with it immortality.

He well recognizes that physical death is but a procedure in existence. Death does not of itself, change the condition of maya, in which the disciple is bound until such a time, as he has earned liberation—mukti, which condition may be defined as immunity from further incarnation.

Immortality is our rightful heritage but it must be claimed,—yea, it must be earned.

It is a mistake to imagine that death makes man immortal. Immortality is an attribute of the gods. But since all souls possess a spark of the divine essence of Brahman (The Absolute), mukti may be attained by earnest seeking, and thus immortality be realized.

This condition of awakening, is variously named among Oriental sages and chelas, such for instance as glimpsing the Brahmic splendor; mutki; samadhi; moksha; entering Nirvana; becoming "twice-born."

In recent years there have come to light in the Occident a number of instances of the attainment of this state, and these have been described as "cosmic consciousness;" "illumination;" "liberation;" the "baptism of the Holy Ghost;" and becoming "immersed in the great white light."

Baptism, which is a ceremony very generally incorporated into religious systems, is a symbol of this esoteric truth, namely the necessity for Illumination in order that the soul may be "saved" from further incarnations—from further experience.

The term cosmic consciousness as well describes this condition of the disciple, as any words can, perhaps, although the term liberation is more literal, since the influx of this state of being, is actually the liberation of the atman, the eternal Self, from the illusion of the external, or maya.

Contrary to the general belief, instances of cosmic consciousness are not extremely rare, although they are not at all general. Particularly is this true in the Orient, where the chief concern as it were, of the people has for centuries been the realization of this state of liberation.

The Oriental initiate in the study of religious practices, realizes that these devotions are for the sole purpose of attaining mukti, whereas in the Occident, the very general idea held by the religious devotee, is one of penance; of propitiation of Deity. This truth applies essentially to the initiate, the aspirant for priesthood, or guru-ship. No qualified priest or guru of the Orient harbors any doubt regarding the object, or purpose of religious practices. The attainment of the spiritual experience described in occidental language as "cosmic consciousness" is the goal.

The goal is not a peaceful death; nor yet an humble entrance into heaven as a place of abode; nor is it the ultimate satisfying of a God of extreme justice; the "eye for an eye" God of the fear-stricken theologian.

One purpose only, actuates the earnest disciple, like a glorious star lighting the path of the mariner on life's troublous sea. That goal is the attainment of that beatific state in which is revealed to the soul and the mind, the real and the unreal; the eternal substance of truth, and the shifting kaleidoscope of maya.

Nor can there be any purpose in the pursuit of either religion or philosophy other than this attainment; nor does the unceasing practice of rites and ceremonies; of contemplation; renunciation; prayers; fasting; penance; devotion; service; adoration; absteminousness; or isolation, insure the attainment of this state of bliss. There is no bartering; no assurance of reward for good conduct. It is not as though one would say, "Ah, my child, if thou wouldst purchase liberation thou shalt follow this recipe."

No golden promises of speedy entrance into Paradise may be given the disciple. Nor any exact rules, or laws of equation by virtue of which the goal shall be reached. Nor yet may any specific time be correctly estimated in which to serve a novitiate, before final initiation.

Many indeed, attain a high degree of spirituality, and yet not have found the key of perfect liberation, although the goal may be not far off.

Many, very many, on earth to-day, are living so close to the borderland of the new birth that they catch fleeting glimpses of the longed-for freedom, but the full import of its meaning does not dawn. There is yet another veil, however thin, between them and the Light.

The Buddha spent seven years in an intense longing and desire to attain that liberation which brought him consciousness of godhood—deliverance from the sense of sin and sorrow that had oppressed him; immunity from the necessity for reincarnation.

Jesus became a Christ only after passing through the agonies of Gethsemane. A Christ is one who has found liberation; who has been born again in his individual consciousness into the inner areas of consciousness which are of the atman, and this attainment establishes his identity with The Absolute.

All oriental religions and philosophies teach that this state of consciousness, is possible to all men; therefore all men are gods in embryo.

But no philosophy or religion may promise the devotee the realization of this grace, nor yet can they deny its possible attainment to any.

Strangely enough, if we estimate men by externalities, we discover that there is no measure by which the supra-conscious man may be measured. The obscure and unlearned have been known to possess this wonderful power which dissolves the seeming, and leaves only the contemplation of the Real.

So also, men of great learning have experienced this rebirth; but it would seem that much cultivation of the intellectual qualities, unless accompanied by an humble and reverent spirit, frequently acts as a barrier to the realization of supra-consciousness.

In "Texts of Taoism," Kwang-Tse, one of the Illuminati, writes:

"He whose mind is thus grandly fixed, emits a heavenly light. In him who emits this heavenly light, men see the true man (i.e., the atman; the Self). When a man has cultivated himself to this point, thenceforth he remains constant in himself. When he is thus constant in himself, what is merely the human element will leave him, but Heaven will help him. Those whom Heaven helps, we call the sons of Heaven. Those who would, by learning, attain to this, seek for what they can not learn."

Thus it will be seen, that according to the reports offered us by this wise man, that which men call learning guarantees no power regarding that area of consciousness which brings Illumination—liberation from enchantment, of the senses—mukti.

Again, in the case of Jacob Boehme, the German mystic, although he left tomes of manuscript, it is asserted authoritatively, that he "possessed no learning" as that word is understood to mean accumulated knowledge.

In "The Spiritual Maxims" of Brother Lawrence, the Carmelite monk, we find this:

"You must realize that you reach God through the heart, and not through the mind."

"Stupidity is closer to deliverance than intellect which innovates," is a phrase ascribed to a Mohammedan saint, and do not modern theologians report with enthusiasm, the unlettered condition of Jesus?

In the Orient, the would-be initiate shuts out the voice of the world, that he may know the heart of the world. Many, very many, are the years of isolation and preparation which such an earnest one accepts in order that he may attain to that state of supra-consciousness in which "nothing is hidden that shall not be revealed" to his clarified vision.

In the inner temples throughout Japan, for example, there are persons who have not only attained this state of consciousness, but who have also retained it, to such a degree and to such an extent, that no event of cosmic import may occur in any part of the world, without these illumined ones instantly becoming aware of its happening, and indeed, this knowledge is possessed by them before the event has taken place in the external world, since their consciousness is not limited to time, space, or place (relative terms only), but is cosmic, or universal.

This power is not comparable with what Occidental Psychism knows as "clairvoyance," or "spirit communication."

The state of consciousness is wholly unlike anything which modern spiritualism reports in its phenomena. Far from being in any degree a suspension of consciousness as is what is known as mediumship, this power partakes of the quality of omniscience. It harmonizes with and blends into all the various degrees and qualities of consciousness in the cosmos, and becomes "at-one" with the universal heart-throb.

A Zen student priest was once discovered lying face downward on the grass of the hill outside the temple; his limbs were rigid, and not a pulse throbbed in his tense and immovable form. He was allowed to remain undisturbed as long as he wished. When at length he stood up, his face wore an expression of terrible anguish. It seemed to have grown old. His guru stood beside him and gently asked: "What did you, my son?"

"O, my Master," cried out the youth, "I have heard and felt all the burdens of the world. I know how the mother feels when she looks upon her starving babe. I have heard the cry of the hunted things in the woods; I have felt the horror of fear; I have borne the lashes and the stripes of the convict; I have entered the heart of the outcast and the shame-stricken; I have been old and unloved and I have sought refuge in self-destruction; I have lived a thousand lives of sorrow and strife and of fear, and O, my Master, I would that I could efface this anguish from the heart of the world."

The guru looked in wonder upon the young priest and he said, "It is well, my son. Soon thou shalt know that the burden is lifted."

Great compassion, the attribute of the Lord Buddha, was the key which opened to this young student priest, the door of mukti, and although his compassion was not less, after he had entered into that blissful realization, yet so filled did he become with a sense of bliss and inexpressible realization of eternal love, that all consciousness of sorrow was soon wiped out.

This condition of effacement of all identity, as it were, with sorrow, sin, and death, seems inseparable from the attainment of liberation, and has been testified to by all who have recorded their emotions in reaching this state of consciousness. In other respects, the acquisition of this supra-consciousness varies greatly with the initiate.

In all instances, there is also an overwhelming conviction of the transitory character of the external world, and the emptiness of all man-bestowed honors and riches.

A story is told of the Mohammedan saint Fudail Ibn Tyad, which well illustrates this. The Caliph Harun-al-Rashid, learning of the extreme simplicity and asceticism of his life exclaimed, "O, Saint, how great is thy self-abnegation."

To which the saint made answer: "Thine is greater." "Thou dost but jest," said the Caliph in wonderment. "Nay, not so, great Caliph," replied the saint. "I do but make abnegation of this world which is transitory, and thou makest abnegation of the next which will last forever."

However, the phrase, "self-abnegation," predicates the concept of sacrifice; the giving up of something much to be desired, while, as a matter of truth, there arises in the consciousness of the Illumined One, a natural contempt for the "baubles" of externality; therefore there is no sacrifice. Nothing is given up. On the contrary, the gain is infinitely great.

Manikyavasayar, one of the great Tamil saints of Southern India, addressed a gathering of disciples thus:

"Why go about sucking from each flower, the droplet of honey, when the heavy mass of pure and sweet honey is available?" By which he questioned why they sought with such eagerness the paltry pleasures of this world, when the state of cosmic consciousness might be attained.

The thought of India, is however, one of ceaseless repudiation of all that is external, and the Hindu conception of mukti, or cosmic consciousness, differs in many respects from that reported by the Illumined in other countries, even while all reports have many emotions in common.

Again we find that reports of the cosmic influx, differ with the century in which the Illumined one lived. This may be accounted for in the fact that an experience so essentially spiritual can not be accurately expressed in terms of sense consciousness.

Far different from the Hindu idea, for example, is the report of a woman who lived in Japan in the early part of the nineteenth century. This woman was very poor and obscure, making her frugal living by braiding mats. So intense was her consciousness of unity with all that is, that on seeing a flower growing by the wayside, she would "enter into its spirit," as she said, with an ecstacy of enjoyment, that would cause her to become momentarily entranced.

She was known to the country people around her as Sho-Nin, meaning literally "above man in consciousness."

It is said that the wild animals of the wood, were wont to come to her door, and she talked to them, as though they were humans. An injured hare came limping to her door in the early morning hours and "spoke" to her.

Upon which, she arose and dressed, and opened the door of her dwelling with words of greeting, as she would use to a neighbor.

She washed the soil from the injured foot, and "loved" it back to wholeness, so that when the hare departed there was no trace of injury.

She declared that she spoke to and was answered by, the birds and the flowers, and the animals, just as she was by persons.

Indeed, among the high priests of the Jains, and the Zens (sects which may be classed as highly developed Occultists), entering into animal consciousness, is a power possessed by all initiates.

Passing along a highway near a Zen temple, the driver of a cart was stopped by a priest, who gently said: "My good man, with some of the money you have in your purse please buy your faithful horse a bucket of oats. He tells me he has been so long fed on rice straw that he is despondent."

To the Occidental mind this will doubtless appear to be the result of keen observation, the priest being able to see from the appearance of the animal that he was fed on straw. They will believe, perhaps, that the priest expressed his observations in the manner described to more fully impress the driver, but this conclusion will be erroneous. The priest, possessing the enlarged or all-inclusive consciousness which in the west is termed "cosmic," actually did speak to the horse.

Nor is this fact one which the western mind should be unable to follow. Science proves the fact of consciousness existing in the atoms composing even what has been termed inanimate objects. How much more comprehensible to our understanding is the consciousness of an animate organism, even though this organism be not more complex than the horse.

There is a Buddhist monastery built high on the cliff overlooking the Japan Inland sea, which is called a "life-saving" monastery.

The priests who preside over this temple, possess the power of extending their consciousness over many miles of sea, and on a vibration attuned to a pitch above the sound of wind and wave, so that they can hear a call of distress from fishermen who need their help.

This fact being admitted, might be accounted for by the uninitiated, as a wonderfully "trained ear," which by cultivation and long practice detects sounds at a seemingly miraculous distance.

But the priests know how many are in a wrecked boat, and can describe them, and "converse" with them, although the fishermen are not aware that they have "talked" to the priest.

Sri Ramakrishna Paramahamsa, the latest incarnation of God in India, and the master to whom the late Swami Vivekananda gives such high praise and devotion, lived almost wholly in that exalted state of consciousness which would appear to be more essentially spiritual, than cosmic in the strict sense of the latter word, since cosmic should certainly imply all-inclusiveness, rather than wholly spiritual (spiritual being here used as an extremely high vibration of the cosmos).

We learn that Sri Ramakrishna was a man comparatively unlettered, and yet his insight was so marvelous, his consciousness so exalted that the most learned pundits honored and respected him as one who had attained unto the goal of all effort—liberation, mukti, while to many persons throughout India to-day, and indeed throughout the whole world, he is looked upon as an incarnation of Krishna.

It is related of Sri Ramakrishna that his yearning for Truth (his mother, he called it), was so great that he finally became unfit to conduct services in the temple, and retired to a little wood near by. Here he seemed to be lost in concentration upon the one thought, to such an extent that had it not been for devoted attendants, who actually put food into his mouth, the sage would have starved to death. He had so completely lost all thought of himself and his surroundings that he could not tell when the day dawned or when the night fell. So terrible was his yearning for the voice of Truth that when day after day passed and the light he longed for had not come to him he would weep in agony.

Nor could any words or argument dissuade him from his purpose.

He once said to Swami Vivekananda:

"My son, suppose there is a bag of gold in yonder room, and a robber is in the next room. Do you think that robber can sleep? He cannot. His mind will be always thinking how he can enter that room and obtain possession of that gold. Do you think, then, that a man firmly persuaded that there is a reality behind all these appearances, that there is a God, that there is One who never dies, One who is Infinite Bliss, a bliss compared with which these pleasures of the senses are simply playthings,—can rest contented without struggling to attain it? No, he will become mad with longing."

At length, after almost twelve years unceasing effort, and undivided purpose Sri Ramakrishna was rewarded with what has been described as "a torrent of spiritual light, deluging his mind and giving him peace."

This wonderful insight he displayed in all the after years of his earthly mission, and he not only attained glimpses of the cosmic conscious state, but he also retained the Illumination, and the power to impart to a great degree, the realization of that state of being which he himself possessed.

Like the Lord Buddha, this Indian sage also describes his experience as accompanied by "unbounded light." Speaking of this strange and overpowering sense of being immersed in light, Sri Ramakrishna described it thus: "The living light to which the earnest devotee is drawn doth not burn. It is like the light coming from a gem, shining yet soft, cool and soothing. It burneth not. It giveth peace and joy."

This effect of great light, is an almost invariable accompaniment of supraconsciousness, although there are instances of undoubted cosmic consciousness in which the realization has been a more gradual growth, rather than a sudden influx, in which the phenomenon of light is not greatly marked.

Mohammed is said to have swooned with the "intolerable splendor" of the flood of white light which broke upon him, after many days of constant prayer and meditation, in the solitude of the cavern outside the gates of Mecca.

Similar is the description of the attainment of cosmic consciousness, given by the Persian mystics, although it is evident that the Sufis regarded the result as reunion with "the other half" of the soul in exile.

The burden of their cry is love, and "union with the beloved" is the longed-for goal of all earthly strife and experience.

Whether this reunion be considered from the standpoint of finding the other half of the perfect one, as exemplified in the present-day search for the soul mate, or whether it be considered in the light of a spiritual merging into the One Eternal Absolute is the question of questions.

Certainly the terms used to express this state of spiritual ecstacy are words which might readily be applied to lovers united in marriage.

One thing is certain, the Sufis did not personify the Deity, except symbolically, and the "beloved one" is impartially referred to as masculine or feminine, even as modern thought has come to realize God as Father-Mother.

In all mystical writings, we find the conclusion that there is no one way in which the seeker may find reunion with The Beloved.

"The ways of God are as the number of the souls of men," declare the followers of Islam, and "for the love that thou wouldst find demands the sacrifice of self to the end that the heart may be filled with the passion to stand within the Holy of Holies, in which alone the mysteries of the True Beloved can be revealed unto thee," is also a Sufi sentiment, although it might also be Christian or Mohammedan, or Vedantan.

Indeed, if the student of Esotericism, searches deeply enough, he will find a surprising unity of sentiment, and even of expression, in all the variety of religions and philosophies, including Christianity.

It has been said that the chief difference between the message of Jesus and those of the holy men of other races, and times, lies in the fact that Jesus, more than his predecessors, emphasized the importance of love. But consider the following lines from Jami, the Persian mystic:

"Gaze, till gazing out of gazing
Grew to BEING HER I gazed on,
She and I no more, but in one
Undivided Being blended.
All that is not One must ever
Suffer with the wound of absence;
And whoever in Love's city
Enters, finds but room for one
And but in Oneness, union."

These lines express that religious ecstacy which results from spiritual aspiration, or they express the union of the individual soul with its mate according to the viewpoint. In any event, they are an excellent description of the realization of that much-to-be-desired consciousness which is fittingly described in Occidental phraseology as "cosmic consciousness." Whether this realization is the result of union with the soul's "other half," or whether it is an impersonal reunion with the Causeless Cause, The Absolute, from which we are earth wanderers, is not the direct purpose of this volume to answer, although the question will be answered, and that soon.

From whence and by whom we are not prepared to say, but the "signs and portents" which precede the solution of this problem have already made their appearance.

Christian students of the Persian mystics, take exception to statements like the above, and regard them as "erotic," rather than spiritual.

Mahmud Shabistari employs the following symbolism, but unquestionably seeks to express the same emotion:

"Go, sweep out the chamber of your heart,
Make it ready to be the dwelling-place of the Beloved.
When you depart out, he will enter in,
In you, void of your_self_, will he display his beauty."

The "Song of Solomon" is in a similar key, and whether the wise king referred to that state of samadhi which accompanies certain experiences of cosmic consciousness, or whether he was reciting love-lyrics, must be a moot question.

The personal note in the famous "song" has been accounted for by many commentators, on the grounds that Solomon had only partial glimpses of the supra-conscious state, and that, in other words, he frequently "backslid" from divine contemplation, and allowed his yearning for the state of liberation, to express itself in love of woman.

An attribute of the possession of cosmic consciousness is wisdom, and this Solomon is said to have possessed far beyond his contemporaries, and to a degree incompatible with his years. It is said that he built and consecrated a "temple for the Lord," and that, as a result of his extreme piety and devotion to God, he was vouchsafed a vision of God.

As these reports have come to us through many stages of church history and as Solomon lived many centuries before the birth of Jesus, it seems hardly fitting to ascribe the raptures of Solomon as typifying the love of the Church (the bride) for Christ (the bridegroom).

Rather, it is easier to believe, the wisdom of the king argues a degree of consciousness far beyond that of the self-conscious man, and he rose to the quality of spiritual realization, expressing itself in a love and longing for that soul communion which may be construed as quite personal, referring to a personal, though doubtless non-corporeal union with his spiritual complement.

Although the pronoun "he" is used, signifying that Solomon's longing was what theology terms "spiritual" and consequently impersonal, meaning God The Absolute, yet we suggest that the use of the masculine pronoun may be due entirely to the translators and commentators (of whom there have been many), and that, in their zeal to reconcile the song with the ecclesiastical ideas of spirituality, the gender of the pronoun has been changed. We submit that the idea is more than possible, and indeed in view of the avowed predilections of the ancient king and sage, it is highly probable.

He sings:

"Let him kiss me with the kisses of his mouth
For his love is better than wine."

Again he cries:

"Behold thou art fair my love, behold thou art fair, thou hast dove's eyes."

The realization of mukti, i.e., the power of the atman to transcend the physical, is thus expressed by Solomon, clearly indicating that he had found liberation:

"My beloved spoke and said unto me, 'Rise up my love my fair one, and come away. For lo, the winter is passed, the rain is over and gone.

"'The flowers appear upon the earth; the time of singing of birds has come, and the voice of the turtle dove is heard in our land.

"'The fig tree putteth forth her green figs, and the vine with the tender grapes gives a goodly smell. Arise my love, my fair one, and come away.'"

It is assumed that these lines do not refer to a personal hegira, but rather to the act of withdrawing the Self from the things of the outer life, and fixing it in contemplation upon the larger life, the supra-conscious life, but there is no reason to doubt that they may refer to a longing to commune with the beautiful and tender things of nature.

Another point to be noted is that in the spring and early summer it is with difficulty that the mind can be made to remain fixed upon the petty details of everyday business life. The awakening of the earth from the long cold sleep of winter is typical of the awakening of the mind from its hypnotisms of external consciousness.

Instinctively, there arises a realization of the divinity of creative activity, and the mind soars up to the higher vibrations and awakes to the real purpose of life, more or less fully, according to individual development.

This has given rise to the assumption, predicated by some writers on cosmic consciousness, that this state of consciousness is attained in the early summer months, and the instances cited would seem to corroborate this assumption.

But, as a poet has sung, "it is always summer in the soul," so there is no specific time, nor age, in which individual cosmic consciousness may be attained.

A point which we suggest, and which is verified by the apparent connection between the spring months, and the full realization of cosmic consciousness, is the point that this phenomenon comes through contemplation and desire for love. Whether this love be expressed as the awakening of creative life, as in nature's springtime, or whether it be expressed as love of the lover for his bride; the dove for his mate; the mother for her child, or as the religious devotee for the Lord, the key that unlocks the door to illumination of body, soul and spirit, is Love, "the maker, the monarch and savior of all," but whether this love in its fullness of perfection may be found in that perfect spiritual mating, which we see exemplified in the tender, but ardent mating of the dove (the symbol of Purity and Peace), or whether it means spiritual union with the Absolute is not conclusive.

The mystery of Seraphita, Balzac's wonderful creation, is an evidence that Balzac had glimpses of that perfect union, which gives rise to the experience called cosmic consciousness.

It is well to remember that in every instance of cosmic consciousness, the person experiencing this state, finds it practically impossible to fully describe the state, or its exact significance.

Therefore, when these efforts have been made, we must expect to find the description colored very materially by the habit of thought, of the person having the experience.

Balzac was essentially religious, but he was also extremely suggestible, and, until very recently, Theology and Religion were supposed to be synonymous, or at least to walk hand in hand. Balzac's early training and his environment, as well as the thought of the times in which he lived, were calculated to inspire in him the fallacious belief that God would have us renounce the love of our fellow beings, for love of Him.

Balzac makes "Louis Lambert" renounce his great passion for Pauline, and seems to suggest that this renunciation led to the subsequent realization of cosmic consciousness, which he unquestionably experienced.

Nor is it possible to say that it did not, since renunciation of the lower must inevitably lead to the higher, and we give up the lesser only that we may enjoy the greater.

In "Seraphita" Balzac expressed what may be termed spiritual love and that spiritual union with the Beloved, which the Sufis believed to be the result of a perfect and complete "mating," between the sexes, on the spiritual plane, regardless of physical proximity or recognition, but which is also elsewhere described as the soul's glimpse of its union with the Absolute or God.

The former view is individual, while the latter is impersonal, and may, or may not, involve absorption of individual consciousness.

In subsequent chapters we shall again refer to Balzac's Illumination as expressed in his writings, and will now take up the question of man's relation to the universe, as it appears in the light of cosmic consciousness, or liberation.

Chapter Two - Man's Relation to God and to His Fellow-Men

The riddle of the Sphinx is no riddle at all. The strange figure, the lower part animal; the upper part human; and the sprouting wings epitomize the growth and development of man from the animal, or physical (carnal), consciousness to the soul consciousness, represented by woman's head and breast, to the supra-conscious, winged god.

No higher conception of life has ever emanated from any source, than the concept of man developed to a state of perfection represented by wings (a symbol of freedom). These winged humans are sometimes called angels and sometimes gods, although the words may not be synonymous.

The point is, that no theory of life and its purposes seems more general or more unescapable than that of man's growth from sin (limitations) to godhood—freedom.

Whether this consummation is brought about through an unbroken chain of upward tendencies from the lowest forms of life to the highest; or whether it is symbolized by the old theologic idea of man's fall from godhood to sin, the fact remains that we know no other ideal than that represented by perfected man; and we know no lower idea than that of man still in the animal stage of consciousness.

Artists, painters, sculptors, wishing to depict the beauty of spiritual things, must still use the human idea for a model—refined, spiritualized, suprahuman, but still man.

It is a truism that man epitomizes the universe. Therefore, the law of growth, which science names evolution, may be studied and applied with equal precision and accuracy to the individual; to a body of individuals called a nation; and to worlds, or planets.

The evolution of an individual is accomplished when he has learned through the various avenues of experience, the fact of his own godhood; and when he has established his union with that indescribable spiritual essence which is called Om; God; Nirvana; Samadhi; Brahm; Kami; Allah; and the Absolute.

A Japanese term is Dai Zikaku. The Zen sect of Japanese Buddhists say Daigo Tettei, and one who has attained to this superior phase of consciousness is called Sho-Nin, meaning literally "above man."

Emerson, the great American seer, expressed this Nameless One, as The Oversoul, and Herbert Spencer, the intellectual giant of England, used the term Universal Energy.

Emerson was a seer; Spencer was a scientist, which word, until recently, was a synonym for materialist.

But what are words?

Mere symbols of consciousness, and subject to change and evolvement, as man's consciousness evolves. The student of truth will recognize in these different words, exactly the same meaning. The "eternal energy from which all things proceed" is a phrase identical with "The Oversoul," or "The Absolute," from which all manifestation comes.

Man's evolution, then, is an evolution in consciousness, from the subjective awareness of the monad to a realization of the entire cosmos.

Each phase of life is a specific degree of consciousness and each successive degree brings the individual nearer to the realization of the sum of all degrees of consciousness, into godhood—the highest degree which we can conceive.

Such, briefly, is a statement of that phenomenon which is attracting the attention of occidental students of psychology, and which has been fittingly termed "the attainment of cosmic consciousness."

The phrase expresses a degree of consciousness which includes the entire cosmos—not only this planet called earth, and everything thereon, but also the spheres of the Constellation.

Not that this degree of consciousness carries with it the power to express in words, that which it is. In fact, the one who has had this marvelous awakening, cannot adequately describe, or even retain, a full comprehension of what it signifies.

All-inclusive knowledge would indeed, preclude the possibility of expression. Therefore, even if it were possible to retain in the finite mind, the full realization of cosmic consciousness, words could not be found in which to express it to others.

Thought is the creator of words, but thought is but the material which the mind employs, and cosmic consciousness transcends the mind, engulfs the soul, and reaches to the trackless areas of Spirit.

It may be doubted if any one may retain a full realization of cosmic consciousness, and remain in the physical body.

Great and wonderful as have been the experiences of those who have sought to relate their sensations, it is probable that these flashes of insight have been in the nature of cosmic perception, and have lacked full realization.

Of those who have had glimpses of that larger area of consciousness which includes an awareness of eternal unity with the cosmos, there are, we believe, many more than students of the subject have any idea of.

This century marks a distinct epoch in what is called evolution.

The end of a kalpa, or cycle of manifestation, is symbolized by the presence on a planet of many avatars, masters, and angels.

By their very presence these enlightened ones arouse in all who are ready for the experience a glimpse of that state of being to which all souls are destined, and to which all shall ultimately attain.

A time when "gods shall walk the earth" is a prophecy which all nations have heard and looked forward to.

That time is now. We see the effect of their presence in Peace Conferences; in abolition of child labor; in prison reform; in the amalgamation of the races; in attempts at social equality; in National Eugenic Societies, and above all, as we have before stated, in the Emancipation of Woman. In fact, it is seen in all the various ways in which the higher consciousness finds expression.

One of the characteristic signs of this awakening, the Millenium Dawn, as it has been named, lies in a very general optimism shining through the mists of doubt and unrest and inexpressible desire, which accompany the new birth in consciousness.

Amid the seeming chaos of present day conditions is it not easy to discern the coming of that dawn of which all great ones of earth have foretold—a time when "the earth shall be made a fit habitation for the gods"?

"The heavens" is a term employed to specify the Constellation which is composed of planets and stars, but we use the term "Heaven" also to mean a state of happiness and bliss attainable through certain methods, a consideration of which we will take up later.

The immediate point is that this planet is being prepared for a position in the solar system consistent with that which is the abode of the gods—Heaven.

This proposition is made in its literal meaning. Corroborative of this statement, which is consistent with all prophecies, is the information recently given to the world, by Camille Flammarion, and other great astronomers, that "the earth is changing its position in the heavens at an astonishing rate." The idea that "there shall be no night there," is foreshadowed by the estimate that this change will give to the earth a perpetual and uniform light, and heat.

The New Thought preachment of physical immortality is but a faint and imperfect perception of this time, when "there shall be no death," because the animal man, subject to change, shall give place to the changeless, deathless, spiritual man; not through cataclysms, and destruction, but through the natural birth into a higher consciousness.

The Occidental mind is easily affrighted by a name. Perhaps we should not specify the Occidental mind, but rather the mind of man among all races is easily put to sleep by the hypnotism of a word.

The word Pantheism is a bugaboo to the Occidentalist. He fears the destruction of the Monistic faith, if he admits that man is in essence a god, and that therefore there are many gods in the one God, even as there are many members to the one physical organism.

Nevertheless all literature, whether sacred or profane, teaches the attainment of godhood by Man. This can not mean other than the attainment of realization of godhood, by the individual and the retention of this realization to the end that reincarnation shall cease and identity with the cosmic, principle, be established, beyond further loss, or doubt, or strife, or death.

This is what it means to attain to cosmic consciousness. It is inclusive consciousness. It is not absorption into the vast unknown, in the sense of annihilation of identity. It is consciousness plus, not minus.

An ancient writing says:

"And thou shalt awake as from a long dream. Thou shalt be like the perfume arising from the flower in which it has been so long enclosed. And thou wilt float above the opened flower. And thou wilt say 'There is time before me in eternity.'"

There is nothing in the testimony of those who have described, as best they could, their emotions upon attainment of this consciousness, which would argue the absorption of the individual soul into The Absolute.

There is no testimony to argue that the attainment of cosmic consciousness, carries with it anything approaching annihilation of sentiency.

Rather it would seem to testify to an acceleration of all the higher faculties.

That this would be a more apt interpretation may be seen by comparing the different reports of those experiencing the phenomenon of Illumination.

Nevertheless there has been much controversy regarding the meaning of the terms nirvana; samadhi; dai zikaku, etc.—words expressing the condition which we are considering under the phrase cosmic consciousness.

What Is Nirvana?

Let us consider briefly, what is meant by Nirvana, and see if it is not highly probable that the word describes the state of consciousness which we are considering, referring later on to the question, and its interpretation by the various schools of religion and philosophy.

It is apparent that the most learned sages of the Orient fail to agree as to the exact meaning of Nirvana. Occidental writers and leaders of the Theosophical philosophy, differ somewhat as to its import, but at the same time we find enough unity on this point to make it evident that the state of Nirvana is a desirable attainment—the goal of the religious enthusiast.

Going back for a moment, to a consideration of the earliest recorded religion of Japan, we find that Sintoism means literally "the way of the gods," meaning the way in which men who have become god-like, found the path that led thereunto, but as to exactly what conditions are represented by godhood, how indeed, is it possible for man to know, much less to express?

Since we are conscious of a divine and irresistible urge toward the attainment of this state of being, it is hardly consistent with what we know of merely human nature, that the way lies in the direction of loss of identity, or in other words, in what is popularly comprehended as absorption. That this idea prevails in many Oriental sects of Buddhism and Vedanta we are aware, but we are confident that this idea is erroneous, and comes from the fact that it is impossible to describe the condition of consciousness enjoyed by the initiate into Nirvana, which term we believe, is identical, or at least comparable with cosmic consciousness.

The very fact that external life represents so universal a struggle for attainment of this state of being, or higher consciousness, indicates at least, even if it does not actually guarantee a fuller, deeper, more complete state of consciousness than hitherto enjoyed, rather than an absorption or annihilation of any of that dearly bought consciousness which distinguishes the self from its environment, and which says with conviction "I am."

It is admitted that those who have experienced liberation, illumination, mukti, have reported their sensations with such relative vagueness and with such apparent variance of conclusion as regards the meaning of the experience that the reader is left to his own interpretation of the character of that state of being, other than a general uniformity of description.

Referring to the pleasure which the lower nature feels under certain conditions, the late Swami Vivekananda says:

"The whole idea of this nature is to make the soul know that it is entirely separate from nature and when the soul knows this, nature has no more attraction for it. But the whole of nature vanishes only for that man who has become free. There will always remain an infinite number of others for whom nature will go on working."

But did Vivekananda employ the phrase "nature has no more attraction for him," to describe the sensation of unappreciativeness of the wonders of the natural world? We think not. Rather the gentle-hearted sage meant to report the fact that the soul is no longer held in bondage to the external world, when it has once attained supra-consciousness.

If this expression referred to the pleasure the true lover of nature feels in the out-of-doors, he might well say "I trust that I shall never attain to that state of consciousness. Or if attainment be compulsory, then shall I prolong the time of accomplishment as long as possible."

And who would blame him? Why should we strive for the attainment of a state of being described so unattractively as to give us the impression of entire loss of so enjoyable and unselfish a sensation as love of nature?

The Vedantic idea, according to interpreted translations is that out of The Absolute, the All (Om), we come, and therefore back to it we go, being now in our present state of consciousness, en route, as it were to return.

But returning to what? That is the unanswerable problem of all religions; all philosophies; all science. If we return to a void, such as some interpreters of the Vedas declare, then surely this urge within mankind toward this annihilatory state would hardly be expected. It would be inconsistent with that instinct of self-preservation which we are told is the first law of nature.

Compared to this Vedantic concept of the Absolute, the Christian's simple, and very empirical ideal of eternal happiness is preferable.

To walk streets paved with gold and play a harp incessantly while chanting doleful praises to a Deity who ought to become wearied of the never-ceasing adulation, would still be a more desirable goal of our strife, than that so inaccurately and unattractively described by many students of Oriental religions and philosophies as the state nirvana, or samadhi.

Again quoting from Vivekananda's Raja Yoga:

"There are not wanting persons who think that this manifest state (our present existence) is the highest state of man. Thinkers of great caliber are of the opinion that we are manifested specimens of undifferentiated Being, and this differentiated state is higher than the Absolute."

Although as Vivekananda says there are thinkers who make this claim, the idea does not find ready acceptance among theologians, either Eastern, or Western. Neither do philosophers, as a general thing incline to adopt this view. The reason for this general disinclination is not difficult of discovery. It is due to the present state of man on this planet.

If man, as we see and know mankind, is the highest state of Being (not merely of manifestation, but of Being) "then," they say, "we have nothing to hope for."

But have we not? May we not hope that man will manifest, on this planet a fuller realization, of that which he is in Being, and that, far from dissolving what consciousness he has, he will but plus this consciousness by a larger— an all-embracing consciousness that shall make earth a fit habitation for godlike men?

In Vivekananda's Raja Yoga we find the following:

"There was an old solution that man, after death, remained the same; that all his good sides, minus his evil sides, remained forever. Logically stated, this means that man's goal is the world; this world meaning earth carried to a state higher and with elimination of its evils is the state they call heaven. This theory, on the face of it, is absurd and puerile because it cannot be. There cannot be good without evil, or evil without good. To live in a world where there is all good and no evil, is what Sanskrit logicians call a 'dream in the air.'"

It is not necessary to argue here that there is no such thing as positive evil.

St. Paul said: "I know and am persuaded that nothing is unclean of itself; save that to him who accounteth anything to be unclean, to him it is unclean."

And again we are assured that "there is nothing good or bad, but thinking makes it so;" which means that evil has no more foundation in reality than has thought, and thought is ever-changing; transitory. Evil therefore may be entirely eliminated by thought, since it is created by thought.

That there is a condition of mankind which has been alluded to as "evil" is self-evident. The term has been employed to describe a condition of either an individual, or a society, or a nation or a race, wherein there is in harmony; disease; unhappiness. Anything that makes for suffering on any plane of consciousness, may be termed "evil" as here used.

Let us consider for a moment if it be illogical to imagine a world in which this in harmony has been eliminated. Imagine a family in which all the members radiate love and unselfish consideration. Add to this, or we may say complementary to this, we have perfect health and prosperity; and over and above all we have a conviction of immortality, eliminating doubt and fear and worry as to future sorrows or partings, with no knowledge that there are others in the world suffering.

Do we not find it quite possible, to say the least, and even desirable, to live in such a family, particularly if we had previously acquired a knowledge of that which is evil and that which is good—merely terms used to describe limited, or enlarged consciousness.

If we admit the desirability of living in such a family, why not in such a world? "Logically stated," says the Hindu swami, "this means that man's goal is this world (earth planet); carried to a state higher and with the elimination of its evils, this world is the state (place) they call heaven."

Again we must question. Why not?

This planet we call earth, is a great and marvelous work, whether it be the work of an abstract God, or whether it be the work of the god in Man.

And whether this earth be the gift of an abstract God, or whether it be the generating bed of the life now upon it, the fact remains that we have no business to despise the gift, or the work of self-generation. Our business is to enhance its beauties and eliminate its ugliness. Why have we prayed that the will of God which is Love, "be done on earth as it is in the heavens," if we despise the planet and hope to leave it?

Although the general impression given in all religious systems is that the perfected soul leaves this earth, yet there is nothing in any of them to prove that it does so, or if it has hitherto, that it shall continue so to do. We have no right to assume that the outer life—the external, manifested life which we perceive with our physical senses, is all there is to this earth and that when we leave this outer life, we go to some other place. The invisible life on this planet is unquestionably far greater than the visible but both visible and invisible doubtless belong to the planet earth.

The Absolute, presumably occupies all space, and therefore it may as reasonably be postulated that this state of Nirvana or Samadhi, may be entered within the area of this planet's vibrations, as in that of the other planets. The finite mind cannot conceive of a state of being apart from motion, space or time, even though these concepts are crude in their relation to the state of consciousness to which the sum of all consciousness is tending, whether the individual would, or not.

We speak of "the heavens" when we refer to the immeasurable, and little known region of the solar system, and we use the same term when we refer to a state of being in which the perfected soul of man will finally enter. And this term implies that when we are thus in heaven, we are with God, if not absorbed into God.

Jesus, the master, taught the coming of the kingdom of God on earth and urged mankind to pray for its coming, asking that the will of God (or gods) be done on earth as it is in the heavens, from which it is not illogical to infer that the earth itself, as a planet, is not outside the pale of that blissful state which we ascribe to God, and which, at the same time, we expect to enter without being swallowed up in the sense that we lose that consciousness which cognizes itself as an eternal verity.

If then, the "heavens" as applied to the planets revolving above the earth in the solar system, and "Heaven" as a term used to describe a state of happiness, bliss, samadhi, nirvana, or "life with God," be synonymous it may reasonably be inferred that in the solar system are planets upon which live sentient beings, in a state to which we on earth, are seeking to attain; a state wherein so-called evil has been eliminated and the good retained.

In fact, we may see with none too prophetic eyes the elimination of evil right here in the visible. All who have attained a glimpse of Illumination have reported the loss of the "sense of sin and death," and have retained this feeling of security and "all-is-well-ness" as long as they have lived thereafter.

From the old conception of "evil" as a positive, opposing and independent force, modern thought, in all its branches, namely science; religion; social evolution, and philosophy, has arrived at the conclusion that evil is not a power or force in and of itself, but that it is evidence of a limited degree of consciousness which sees only one side of a subject—only a limited area of an infinitely wide and varied manifestation of the one supreme consciousness. Therefore, it is, that evil per se, does not exist as power, but that it is the effect of a misapplication of power.

The cure then, for this state of Relativity, is found logically enough, in an extension of individual consciousness.

That this idea is logical may be deduced from the fact that as the mind expands, through the various channels of learning; observation; contact with each other, and by the many roads of Experience, altruism becomes more general. Almost every one readily admits that the world is "growing better," as they express it.

This means that the individual consciousness is becoming broadened, deepened, enlarged; and this enlargement makes it possible to show that the happiness of each one, means the happiness of all, and that no one human life can reach the goal of freedom and eternal life (mukti, which can mean nothing less than godhood) unless he does so by some one of the many paths of selflessness.

Up through the perilous paths and the devious ways of brute consciousness toward a more or less perfect perception of that blissful state which the Illumined have sought to describe, each individual has come to his present state; and it is only by virtue of the ability to look back over the path, and to look onward a little into relative futurity, that each may record the fact of his gain in consciousness, and what this gain means to the future of this earth.

But who is there who cannot see that each step in attainment of consciousness brings with it a corresponding freedom from suffering?

The planet itself does not make us suffer. The latest discoveries of astronomers indicate that as the standard of morality (using the term "morality" in its true sense), becomes higher, the position of the earth itself becomes changed, in its relation to the solar system.

In this way, it is expected that a uniform temperature will prevail all over the earth's surface; and with the cessation of war, and of competition (which is mental warfare) cataclysms, storms, and earthquakes will cease. When we come, as we will, in succeeding chapters of this book, to a review of the experiences of those who have attained cosmic consciousness (mukti) we will find that, in each instance, there has come a realization of the nothingness of sin and consequent suffering.

The trouble then, is not with the earth as a planet, but with the lack of consciousness of earth's inhabitants, which lack makes possible all the suffering which afflicts human life.

Those who have attained to the state of cosmic consciousness in both Occidental and Oriental instances of this perception, have reported an abiding sense of rest and peace and satisfaction—a condition which we associate with accepted ideals of heaven as taught in Occidental creeds and among some schools of Oriental philosophers, and sects of religious worship.

There is a far greater unity of idea between the Oriental and the Occidental methods and systems, as to the goal of ultimate attainment than is generally believed, or understood.

The highest expression of Japanese Buddhism differs from Hindu Buddhism and from Vedanta, and the many other forms of Hindu philosophy and religion, in the same way that the Japanese, as a nation, differ from their Hindu brothers.

The Japanese emphasize, more than do the Hindus, the preservation of the nation, and to this end, they are called more "practical" minded, but with the Japanese, as with all the Orientals, we find an intense contempt for any one who would seek to preserve his physical existence, or hesitate at any personal sacrifice.

This unwritten code has its origin, as have all Oriental traditions and concepts, in the teachings of religious systems. According to Oriental ethics, the person is very low in the scale of consciousness, when he considers his physical body as of comparative consequence, when the question of expediency, or of the welfare of his country, is in the balance.

Nevertheless, Japan has offered, far more than has India, a fertile field for the growth of materialism, owing to the fact that underlying the apparent observance of and loyalty to, religious practices, the Japanese temperament inclines to a practical application of the wisdom attained through religious instruction.

Therefore we find among the Illumined Ones of Japanese history, sages who taught the attainment of liberation through paths which are not generally accepted by interpreters of Hinduism.

For example, among the orthodox Sintoists, (the original religion of the Japanese, before the advent of Buddhism), we find that cleanliness of mind and body, was taught as the prime essential to attainment of unity with Kami, rather than contemplation, meditation and isolation, as with the Hindus.

And in the Christian world we have a corresponding admonition in the phrase "cleanliness is next to godliness."

Simple as this rule of conduct is, it nevertheless embodies the key to the situation, inasmuch as we are assured that "blessed are the pure in heart for they shall see God."

Again Jesus told his hearers that they "must become as little children," evidently meaning that they must possess the clean, pure, guileless mind of a little child, if they would reach the goal of liberation, from strife; death (repeated incarnation); and all so-called "evil."

To this end man is striving, whether by rites and ceremonies of religion; by worship; by contemplation; by effort and struggle; by invention; by aspiration; by sacrifice; or by whatever path, or device, or system.

What, then is the goal, and how may it be attained?

Before taking up this question, let us go back a little over the history of human life and attainment, and trace, briefly, the evolution of consciousness, from pre-historic man, to the highest examples of human devotion and wisdom, of which, happily, the world affords not a few instances.

Chapter Three - Areas of Consciousness

Consciousness may be termed, simply, "the divine spark," which enters into every form and phase of manifested life emanating from that one Eternal Power which materialists designate as "energy" and which Occultists, both Oriental and Occidental, best define as "Aum," God! The Absolute—The Divine Mind, and many other terms.

Consciousness, therefore, enters into everything—is the life essence of everything.

The materialistic hypothesis formerly predicated the axiom that there were two distinct phases of manifestation, namely organic and inorganic.

Organic life was sentient, or conscious, while inorganic life was insensate—a structure acted upon from forces outside itself, and dependent upon an exterior force for its action.

Other names for this differentiation, would be "matter" and "spirit." The point is, that the old materialistic philosophy failed to recognize the fact that consciousness, in varying degrees, characterizes all manifested life.

This fact every phase of Oriental philosophy recognized, and always has recognized. The assumption of the Christian Science devotee, that there is anything new in the postulate that "all is spirit," is possible only because of his ignorance of Oriental philosophy, as will be seen later on in these pages, when we take up the relative comparison between the Oriental and the Occidental systems of "salvation."

To resume therefore, we postulate the following recognized axioms of Universal Occultism.

All life is sentient or conscious.

All life is from the one source, and therefore contains this "divine spark."

All manifestation expresses degrees or phases of consciousness.

The degree of this consciousness fixes the status of the organism, and determines its classification, whether it is organic or inorganic; simple, or complex.

Every cell, each separate cell, in fact, has its own consciousness—that is each cell is a center of this power that we term consciousness; a group of cells with this power focalized to a given point, or center, makes an organ of consciousness, and so on up the scale through many many degrees of complexity of organism, until we come to man.

Webster defines consciousness as "the ability to know ones mental operations." But, we do not take this definition in Occultism, for the obvious reason, that it is not possible to state arbitrarily whether or not, the cell "knows its operations," and since all operations are necessarily mental in the final analysis, we assume that there is a phase of consciousness below that of cognition of "self," which may be termed "the unconscious consciousness," which again is synonymous with the phrase "automatic cerebration."

Coming up through the various myriad degrees of sub-conscious life (sub being here used as below self consciousness) we arrive at the stage of simple consciousness which characterizes the animal kingdom, remembering that consciousness in the abstract is not a condition, or state of environment. It is one of the eternal verities. It is just as Aum is.

The attainment of a wider and wider area of consciousness, is but the uncovering, or the attracting to a central point or to an individual organism of this that is. Thus consciousness, in the abstract, may say of itself "before creation was, I am."

That is what is meant when it is said that God is omnipotent, and omniscient.

The difference between mere power, or energy, and consciousness, whether considered from the standpoint of the organic or the inorganic kingdom, may be likened to the difference between a blind force, and a power that knows itself.

Consciousness is practically the great central light that "lighteth every man that cometh into the world." Without consciousness, manifestation would be darkness. Thus it is said, "the light shineth in darkness and the darkness comprehendeth it not." This applies to that tiny spark of divinity in which consciousness exists but where there is not realization of its divinity.

This fact is not applicable to the inorganic, or the animal kingdoms alone. Many men are not conscious of the light that shineth within them, save as there is an aggregate of cell consciousness which recognizes its focalized power as an organism.

Manifestation then, is the vehicle (carrying character) of universal consciousness, and we may logically assume that manifestation is due to the necessity of developing individualized entities, who may, through successive phases of conscious unfoldment, or uncovering of areas of Being, become gods.

The western writers, and indeed, many Oriental seers prefer to put it thus: "become fit to dwell with God, in eternal bliss and power."

To dwell with God, must be to become gods. Once more, we must remember that only gods are immortal. Souls continue to exist after the physical body has been discarded, for the reason that no body in these days, lives as long as its psychic counterpart or dweller. But, although the soul continues to exist on another plane of note of the scale of vibration, it does not argue that the identity shall continue eternally, except in such instances, as when the soul through numbers of incarnations shall have finally accomplished the purpose of its pilgrimage and attained to mukti (liberation from the law of change and death).

Returning to a consideration of what may be said to constitute certain specific phases of consciousness, we will take into consideration the phase of consciousness, which we see expressed in the mineral kingdom. That there is a distinct and separate character of consciousness thus expressed is evident from the fact that there is a law of chemical affinity, i.e. attraction and repulsion, which causes different minerals to respond, or to refuse to respond, as the case may be, to certain conditions or chemical processes, more or less crude in character.

From this to the vegetable kingdom we assume a step in advance, as vegetable life measured by complexity and refinement, responds with a greater degree of sensitiveness to the laws of evolution, as expressed in cultivation, selection and environment.

Even in this phase of manifestation, we find the law of Being, is measured by the perfection of species. Evolution of inorganic life, is as real, and as much a part of the plan, (or whatever name we choose), as is organic, and self-conscious life.

That which is less perfect, measured by the law of beauty and usefulness, we find gradually being exterminated. That the earth, as a planet, is obeying this cosmic law of evolution from grossness to refinement; from crudity to perfection; from the limited to the all-inclusive, is indisputable. As the motor power of electricity has become general, we find that beasts of burden are fast disappearing from the earth, according to the law of the "survival of the fittest," this law, always being subject to change. The "fittest" means that which is best fitted to the conditions of the time.

Brute force survives among brutes, in the degree that it is strong or weak; coming out of that expression of law into the mental areas of consciousness, we find that the mentally fit survive among those who live only in the areas of the mind; so on, into the spiritual, we will find the "survival of the fittest" will be those who are best fitted for spiritual eternity—for godhood.

Coming again, to our consideration of the term consciousness, we will take a brief survey of that phase of consciousness which we see manifested in the forms of life that have the power to move from their immediate environment; such for instance would include the fish in the sea; insect life; reptiles; the birds in the air; and all forms of animal life.

While expressing a very limited degree of consciousness, yet there is evident a certain degree or aggregate of cell consciousness, which transcends that of the mineral and vegetable life. This apparently advanced degree of consciousness, does not, as we have stated, presuppose a nearer approach to immortality, however, for the reason that we apply the law of the survival of the fittest to all manifestation, and that which is best fitted for certain stages of the planet's life during the process of evolvement, may be most unfitted for succeeding stages, and will, by the inexorable law of survival, be discontinued—discarded, even as the properties and stage-settings of a drama are thrown aside, when the play has been "taken off the boards."

It is admitted, therefore, that those forms of life having the power of locomotion, involve a more complex degree of consciousness, than does that of the mineral or vegetable.

In that phase of life that we see possessing the power to move, to change its immediate environment, even though not capable of changing its habitat we may perceive the beginning of that consciousness expressed as "free-will." Here, we assume, the organism recognizes its self as distinct from its environment, and from its counterparts, etc., but this recognition has not sufficient consciousness to assert that recognition, and so we say that there is no self-consciousness. There is what occultists have agreed to call simple consciousness, but this does not include a realization of identity, as apart from environment. This may be better understood if we separate these degrees or phases of consciousness into groups, applicable to the human organism, leaving, for a time the consideration of whether or not some human specimens are higher in the scales than are some animals.

Physical, or sense consciousness, is shared alike by man and the animals.

Beyond this phase of consciousness we may classify the human species in the following terms:

Physical self-consciousness.

Mental self-consciousness.
Soul (individual) "I" consciousness.
Spiritual self-consciousness.

Physical self-consciousness is that phase of self-recognition which knows itself as a body distinct from its neighbors; from its natural environment. This awareness of the self it is that actuated pre-historic man when he manifested the blind force that is sometimes called "self-preservation," which force has erroneously been termed "the first law of nature."

Preservation of this physical self is the most "primitive" law of nature, but not "first" in the sense that it is the most important, or the strongest.

The world's long list of heroes refutes this idea. The pre-historic species of human, then, in common with his brother, the animal, sought to preserve this physical self, because he felt that this physical self, his body, was all there was of him, and he wished to preserve it, even as the wise man of to-day, sacrifices everything to the preservation of the moral and spiritual Self which he realizes is the real of him.

To this end, he cultivated physical force, sufficient to overcome his environment; and as he developed a little of that consciousness which we term mental (using the term merely as a part of the physical organism called the brain), he realized that co-operation would greatly enhance his chances for self-preservation, and therefore, this mental consciousness impelled him to annex to his forces other physical organisms so that their united strength might preserve each other.

This side of the story of man's evolution in consciousness is not however a part of our present work, and we will therefore leave it, for a brief consideration of the successive steps in attainment of consciousness, leading through devious paths, and through millions of relative time called years, into the present state of man's consciousness which in so many instances presages the oncoming of that state, called liberation, or illumination—mukti.

Through mental self-consciousness the way has been long and arduous. There are many, many degrees of this phase of consciousness, and to this phase we owe what is called our present civilization.

The true occultist, whether viewing manifestation from the standpoint of Oriental or of Occidental ideals, realizes that everything is right which makes for human betterment, and that dharma (right-action) consists in acting in accordance with the highest motive of which one's consciousness is capable.

That our present civilization is most uncivilized in many respects, will be admitted by all whose range of consciousness has touched in any degree, the infinite areas of wisdom expressed in altruistic action.

But, though the path be long, and thorny, the cycle is closing, and many have reached the goal through its zigzag course.

But, underlying, as it were, and upholding and uplifting the expression of sense consciousness in which so many persons seem lost to-day, there are evidences of a consciousness which observes the effects, of this tremendous mental activity, and knows itself as something apart from, and superior to this manifestation.

This, we define as soul—individualized expression of the spiritual consciousness—the central light, which as we previously quoted, "lighteth every man that cometh into the world."

Many there are who merely perceive this. To them there is a vague and indefinable something which seems to realize that the operations of the mind are something phenomenal and apart from the real Self. Psychology, even so empirical a psychology as is possible of demonstration in western schools and colleges, evidences the fact that there is a far greater field of mental operation than is covered by the outer, or mental consciousness.

The outer, or objective action of the mind, considers but one subject, one question, one problem at a time. Many varied phases of this problem may present themselves, but the mental forces are focalized upon one subject at a time. And yet to state that but one idea, thought-concept, or desire, can enter the mind at a time, is not a safe assumption.

After many centuries of material strife, with the object of satisfying the demands of human life, the conviction is forcing itself upon people in all walks of life, that wealth, ambition, power and possessions, do not give us the answer to the eternal unescapable and insistent question of the way to happiness.

This means that there is awakening in the human race more generally than at any other time in recorded history, a realization that the human organism is not merely a physical aggregate of cells, nor yet that it is mind individualized and in operation for the purpose of exercising new powers. The fact is becoming apparent that all discovery is but an uncovering of those vast areas of consciousness which are limitless; and which include not only all life on this planet, but all life in the Cosmos. In short, cosmic consciousness is becoming perceived, by a vast majority, and is being realized by not a few.

But in the immediate future of the race, we find the next step, for the majority to be that of soul-consciousness.

Back of thought, like a guardian angel stands the desire of the soul, stimulating and directing; back of action stands thought, as the master directs the servant, or as the captain decides the course of the ship.

Spiritual evolution may be understood, or at least perceived, from a study of physical and mental evolution. From the crude to the perfect is the law; if this perfection of species, or of phases, could be attained without pain, it were well. Pain comes from lack of wisdom to realize that out of the lower the higher inevitably springs, as the butterfly springs from the cocoon; as the flower springs from the seed; "as above so below" is a translation of an old Sinto saying, which also bids us "trust in Kami and keep clean."

Again it is said "to him who overcometh, will I give the inheritance." Overcoming may be variously interpreted. In the past, it has been presented to the initiate, as sacrifice. If so it be, then is it because of lack of that wisdom which knows that there is no sacrifice in exchanging the physical for the spiritual—the ephemeral for the abiding.

Says the ancient manuscripts:

"The body is purified by water, the mind by truth, the soul by knowledge and austerity, the reason by wisdom."

But as the groping, undeveloped soul struggles for consciousness, it reaches out for the gratification of mental desires. The soul is moved by desire for perfect happiness. The mind seeks to satisfy this craving for happiness in increased activities; in accumulation; in so-called pleasure, i.e. always looking outside—thinking outside, living in the outside—the maya. But the soul has but one answer to this quest for happiness. It is love, because only love and wisdom give immortality—which is self-preservation in the true sense.

It is written in the Shruti: "Brahman is wisdom and bliss."

No higher text can be given the disciple.

Wisdom comes from reflection upon the results of Experience, in the search for happiness.

When the mind has sounded the depths of its resources, and the urge forward can not be appeased, when the voice of the inner self—the soul, cannot be silenced; the disciple pauses to ask the way. He wants to know what it is all about, and why it is that all he has so striven and struggled for fails to satisfy. He wants to know how to avoid pain; and how to find the most direct road to that satisfaction which endures; and which is not synonymous with the so-called "pleasures" of the senses.

When this stage of development has been reached, the disciple is ready for another phase of Experience which shall extend his consciousness into those areas of knowledge, in which the Real is distinguishable from the Illusory.

Experience will then teach him that only Love is real.

That which is for the permanent good of all, as opposed to that which is transitory and only seemingly satisfying to the few, may be said to constitute the perception of the Real, and the avoidance of Illusion.

To exchange a present seeming advantage to the physical environment, for a future and permanent satisfaction of the soul is the prerogative of the wise—the soul that has discovered itself and its mission.

In all organisms below the scale of the human, there is a constant growth in complexity of organism, with specialization of functions.

When we come to this last-mentioned stage of human development, we find that there is no more specialization in the way of development of the physical functions. Instead, there is a determined effort at perfecting the higher functions, through the gradations of consciousness, until the spiritual consciousness of the individual entity has been awakened.

Then, indeed, has been awakened the "divine man" and the path to immortality is henceforth comparatively short, although by no means strewn with roses, judged from the limited standard of Relativity.

A man's karma simply and mathematically, proves the direction of his former desires. Karma does not punish or reward, as is frequently imagined.

The general impression that one is reaping "good or bad karma" according as his life is one of pleasure or of pain, is not the solution of the problem of karma, and has no relation to the law of karmic action.

If a soul has in a previous life outgrown or outworn that evolutionary phase of development, in which the mind seeks temporary pleasures, and has come to the place where he wants to distinguish the Real from the Illusory, his karma, in compliance with the law of desire, will bring him in relation to those conditions which will teach him to know the Real from the Illusory, and in those conditions he will experience pain because he will, if he remain in the activities of the world, be acting contrary to the ideas of the average.

Thus, to the onlooker, and in accordance with the general misinterpretation of the law of karma, he will be thought to have reaped a "bad" karma, while as a matter of reality, he will be making very rapid strides on the path to godhood. Said a famous Japanese high priest:

"Desire is the bird that carries the soul to the object in which his mind is immersed, and thus his future actions are the result."

This means that by the law of desire, acting in accordance with the evolutionary pilgrimage of the soul, the karma is produced. The American poet, Lowell, says: "No man is born into the world whose work is not born with him." However, whether or not this applies to man in the first stages of his upward climb to the goal of attainment of conscious godhood, it most assuredly applies to those souls who have become aware of their purpose, and who have made a conscious choice of their karma. And of this class of souls, the world to-day has a goodly number.

The end of a kalpa finds many avatars, and angels on earth, and however obscured the mind of these may become in the fog of Illusion, the inner light guides them through its mists to the safe accomplishment of their mission.

There is a story of a Buddhist priest, who when dying, was comforted by his loving disciples with the reminder that he was at last entering upon a state of bliss and rest. To which the earnest one replied:

"Never so long as there is misery to be assuaged, shall I enter Nirvana. I shall be reborn where the need is greatest. I shall wish to be reborn in the nethermost depths of hell, because that is the place that most needs enlightenment; that is the place to point out the path to deliverance; that is the place where the light will shine most brightly."

Thus it will be seen we may not readily determine what is "good" and what is "bad" karma, by judging from external conditions.

As we are told that we may entertain "angels unawares," so we may pass the world's avatars upon the street, and judging from the external, the physical environment, we may not know them from the vampire souls that contact them.

The point of our present consideration is that this "year of grace," meaning not the mere twelve months of the calendar year, but the century, is the end of the present kalpa (cycle), and demonstrates that period of evolution has terminated, and the era is at hand when spiritual alchemy shall transform the old into the new, and that the desire, which has so long ministered to the wants of the physical body, shall be turned (converted) into the channels that lead to spiritual consciousness.

The undefined, instinctive urge that has actuated so many intrepid souls, is becoming recognized for what it is—the awakening of the inner Self; the blind groping in the dark will cease and there shall arise a race of human beings liberated; free; aware of their spiritual origin and their inherent divinity.

All who have conformed their life activities to the divine law of action, which may be tersely stated as "Not mine, but thine, dear brother," will have achieved the goal of the soul's purpose—will have found Nirvana.

Chapter Four - Self-Ness and Selflessness

During what is historically known as the Dark Ages, the esoteric meaning of religious practices became obscured. This is true no less, and no more, of Oriental countries, than of European. The long night through which the earth passed during that time and since, but foreshadowed a coming dawn. In the still very imperfect light of the dawning day, truth is seen but dimly, and its rays appear distorted, whereas, when seen with the "pure and spotless eye" they are straight and clear and simple.

Indeed, the very simplicity of Truth causes her to pass unnoticed.

While to the superficial observer; the student who is mentally eager but who lacks the wonderful penetrating power of spiritual insight, there seems to be a great complexity in Oriental philosophy, the fact is, that the entire aggregation of systems is simple enough when we have the key.

One of the stumbling blocks; the inexplicable enigma to many Occidental students, is the problem of the preservation, of the Self, and the constant admonition to become selfless. The two appear paradoxical.

How may the Self acquire consciousness and yet become selfless?

Throughout the Oriental teachings, no matter which of the many systems we study, we find the oft-repeated declaration that liberation can never be accomplished and Nirvana reached, by him "who holds to the idea of self."

It is this universally recognized aphorism which has given rise to the erroneous conception of Nirvana as absorption of all identity.

Hakuin Daisi, the St. Paul of Japanese Buddhism, cautioned his disciples that they must "absorb the self into the whole, the cosmos, if they would never die," and Jesus assured his hearers that "he who loses his life for my sake shall find it."

Christians have taken this simple statement to mean that he who endured persecution and death because of his espousal of Christianity, would be rewarded in the way that a king bestows lands and titles, for defense of his person and throne.

This is the limited viewpoint of the personal self; it is far from being consistent with the wisdom of the Illumined Master.

He who has sufficient spiritual consciousness to desire the welfare of all, even though his own life and his own possessions were the price therefore, can not lose his life. Such a one is fit for immortality and his godhood is claimed by the very act of renunciation—not as a reward bestowed for such renunciation.

By the very act of willingness to lose the self we find the Self. Not the self of externality. Not the self that says "I am a white man; or a black man; or a yellow man; or a red man." That says "I am John Smith"—or any other name. The awareness of this kind of selfhood, this personal self, is like looking at one's reflection in the mirror and saying, "Ah, I have on a becoming attire," or "my face looks sickly to-day." It is the same "I" that looked yesterday and found the face looking excellently well, so that there must have been consciousness behind the observation, that could take cognizance of the difference in appearance of yesterday's reflection and that which met that cognizing eye today.

Eagerness to retain consciousness of the personal self blocks the way of Illumination which uncovers the real, the greater, the higher Self—the atman.

This constant adjuration to sink the self into The Absolute, is what has given rise to so much difference of interpretation as to the meaning of mukti, liberation. It sounds paradoxical to state that it is only by giving up all consciousness of self, that immortal Self-hood is gained.

Thus has arisen all the confusion as to the meaning of "absorption into a state of bliss." How may the Self realize a state of selflessness and yet not be lost in a sea of un consciousness?

Only one who is capable of self-sacrifice were he called upon, can correctly answer this question, and by what may be termed the very law of equation, the sacrifice becomes impossible.

Should any one seek to bargain with himself to pay the price of loss of self, so that he might gain the higher, fuller life, his sacrifice would be in vain because it would not be selflessness, but selfishness—there could be no sacrifice, were it a bargain.

Let no one think that this unchanging law of the Cosmos is in the nature of either reward or punishment, or that it was devised by the gods, as a method of initiation—a test of fitness for Nirvana. Even though the test be applied by the gods, it is not of their planning.

It is, just as the absolute is, and analysis of the way and wherefrom is not possible of contemplation.

If it sometimes appears that Illumined Ones have seemed to infer a loss of identity of the Self, it should be remembered that not only have these reported instances of liberation (cosmic consciousness attained), been vague, but they have necessarily suffered from the impossibility of describing that which is indescribable. We should also remember that translators employ the words in the English language which most nearly express their interpretation of the original meaning.

Words are at best but clumsy symbols.

Perfect bliss is voiceless—inexpressible.

This does not, however, mean that perfect bliss is nothingness. Rather is it everything-ness, in that it is all-embracing in its realization. In complete realization of the Cosmos nothing is excluded. Exclusiveness is a concomitant of the state of consciousness pertinent to the personal self, which state is not excluded from the consciousness described as cosmic, nirvana or mukti, but on the contrary, is included in it, even as the simple vibrations of the musical scale are included in the great harmonies of Wagner's compositions.

"He who has realized Brahman becomes silent," says Ramakrishna. "Discussions and argumentations exist so long as the realization of The Absolute does not come. If you melt butter in a pan over a fire, how long does it make a noise? So long as there is water in it. When the water is evaporated it ceases to make further noise. The soul of the seeker after Brahman may be compared to fresh butter. Discussions and argumentations of a seeker are like the noise caused during the process of purification by the fire of knowledge. As the water of egotism and worldliness is evaporated and the soul becomes purer, all noise of debates and discussions ceases and absolute silence reigns in the state of samadhi."

A better translation of the word "noise" would be "sputtering."

Sound is not necessarily noise. The idea conveyed is not intended to be a condition in which the soul becomes anæsthetized as it were, but a state of knowing, and the effort and the sputtering of questioning and searching is passed.

The same gospel better expresses the meaning thus:

"The bee buzzes so long as it is outside the lotus, and does not settle down in its heart to drink of the honey. As soon as it tastes of the honey all buzzing is at an end. Similarly all noise of discussion ceases when the soul of the neophyte begins to drink the nectar of Divine Love, at the lotus feet of the Blissful One."

Who will not say that the bee is more satisfied when he has found and drank of the honey than when he is buzzingly seeking it?

Surely it is not necessary to be of one mind, in order that we may be of one heart. Even though we were as "like as two peas in a pod," it is well to note that the two peas are two spheres—nature has made them separate and distinct despite their close resemblance.

To unite with the absolute should correspond to this unity of all hearts in the desire for a common effort to establish harmony, while we permit to each individual the freedom of mind; of taste; of choice of pursuits; of choice of pleasure; of discrimination; and preservation of identity.

Our contention is that mukti, or liberation (which we believe to be identical with attainment of cosmic consciousness) does not mean an absorption into the Universal, the Absolute, Brahm, to the extent of annihilation of identity.

And we claim that this view finds corroboration in the best interpretation of Oriental philosophies and religions, as well as in the Christian doctrine.

Says Nagasena, the Buddhist sage:

"He who is not free from passion experiences both the taste of food, and also the passion due to that taste; while he who is free from passion experiences the taste of food but no passion."

Hence we discover that the state of Illumination, samadhi, or mukti, according to the most enlightened and logical interpretation, means a calm and peaceful consciousness, undisturbed by passion. But we should not interpret the word "passion" as here used, to mean absence of all sensation, feeling or knowledge.

There is absolutely no arbitrary interpretation or translation of the words of Buddha, nor can there be. The same is true of Confucius; of Mohammed; of Krishna; of Laotze; of Jesus; of all the teachers and philosophers of the world.

Who of you who read these words has not listened to debates and endless discussions as to what even so modern a writer as Emerson or Whitman, or Nietzsche or Kobo Daisi, or some other, may have meant by certain statements?

In the Samyutta Nikaya we read:

"Let a man who holds the Self clear, keep that Self free from wickedness."

This does not imply annihilation of identity, absorption of consciousness, although it has been so interpreted by many students. On the contrary, instead of losing consciousness of the Self (which is not merely the personality), we find the Real Self.

As an adult we realize more consciousness than we do as infants. Not that we possess more consciousness. We cannot acquire consciousness as we accumulate things. We can not add one iota to the sum of consciousness, but we can and do uncover portion upon portion of the vast area of consciousness which is.

Says the Dhammapada:

"As kinsmen, friends and lovers salute a man who has been long away and returns safe from afar; in like manner his good deeds receive him who has done good, and who has gone from this world to the other, as kinsmen receive a friend on his return."

If this state of mukti were annihilation of individual consciousness it would hardly be an incentive to do good deeds, except that good deeds in themselves bring happiness, but if the bringing of happiness did not also bring with it a larger consciousness, it would not be true happiness, but merely a condition, and conditions are always subject to change.

"It is not separateness you should hope and long for; it is union—the sense of oneness with all that is, that has ever been and that can ever be—the sense that shall enlarge the horizon of your being, to the limits of the universe; to the boundaries of time and space; that shall lift you up into a new plane far beyond, outside all mean and miserable care for self. Why stand shrinking there? Give up the fool's paradise of 'This is I'; 'This is mine.' It is the great reality you are asked to grasp. Leap forward without fear. You shall find yourself in the ambrosial waters of Nirvana and sport with the Arhats who have conquered birth and death."

This admonition to give up the struggle and strife for separateness is interpreted by many to declare for annihilation of consciousness of identity, but we contend that union is in no wise akin to annihilation, and since this assurance of union is further described as an enlargement of the horizon of your being, it is evident that your being can not be enlarged by becoming annihilated, or even absorbed into The Absolute, as in that event it would cease to be your being. Moreover, you are told that you will "sport with the Arhats who have conquered birth and death." Arhats are alluded to in the plural, and not as One Being.

To be sure there may be a final state of absorption of consciousness far beyond this state of being which is described as Nirvana.

Theosophy lays much stress upon the assumption that the attainment of godhood is possible to every human soul, but that this godhood must inevitably have an ultimate conclusion. That is, there is a place or heaven, which is called the Devachanic plane, and this plane, or place, is inhabited by "gods," for a definite period, approximating thousands of years, but that the final conclusion must be, absorption of identity into the universal reservoir of mind, or consciousness. But we may readily see that beyond the Devachanic plane, we may not penetrate with the limited consciousness which takes cognizance of external conditions. Any attempt, therefore, at a description of what occurs to the individual consciousness beyond the areas of Devachan, must be futile.

The argument that most logically postulates the assumption that all identity, or differentiation of consciousness, becomes absorbed into The Absolute, is based upon the fact that we remember nothing of previous states of consciousness. That is, the devious pathway by which the advanced and progressive individual has reached his present state or realization of consciousness, is shrouded in oblivion. From this it is not unnatural to assume that since we have come OUT OF THE VOID, having apparently no memory or realization of what preceded this coming, we will return to the same state, when we shall have completed the round of evolution.

This postulate, is, however, merely the result of our limited power of comprehension, and may or may not be true. The answer is as yet inexplicable to the finite mind, considered from the standpoint of relative proof.

If it were a fact, that all Oriental sages experiencing the phenomenon of liberation, mukti, had reported what would seem to be annihilation of identity of consciousness, we still maintain that this fact would not be proof sufficient upon which to postulate this conclusion, for the very obvious reason that the present era promises what Occidental theology, science, and philosophy unite in designating as a "new dispensation," wherein the "old shall pass away," and a "new order" shall be established.

"Look how the fine and valuable gold-dust shifts through the screen, leaving only the useless stones and debris in the catches; even so that which is infinitely fine substance becomes lost when sifted through the screen of the limited mind of man," said a wise Japanese high priest.

However, it is our contention that Buddhism, far indeed from postulating the assumption that individual consciousness is swallowed up in The Absolute, as is frequently understood by Occidental translators of Buddhistic writings, announces a calm and unquestioning conviction in the power of man to attain to immortality, and consequent godhood, through contemplation of faith in his own identity with the Supreme One.

When we consider that there are in the religion of Buddhism, as many as sixty different expositions of the teachings of the Lord Buddha, and that these vary, even as the Christian sects vary in their interpretations and presentments of the instructions of the Master, Jesus of Nazareth, we begin to have some idea of the difficulties of correct interpretation of the obscure and mystical language in which mukti is ever described.

One of the most quoted of the translations of the Life of Buddha, reaches the English readers through devious ways, namely, from the Sanskrit into Chinese, and from the Chinese into English, and again edited by an English scientist who is also an Oriental scholar.

We must also consider the poverty of the English language when used to describe supra-conscious experiences, or what modern thought terms Metaphysics. Only within very recent times, approximating twenty-five years, there have been coined innumerable words in the English language.

The advances made in mechanical, scientific, ethical and philosophical thought, have made this a necessity, while, when it comes to an attempt at clarifying the meaning of mystical terms, a very wide range of interpretation is imperative.

Buddha, addressing his servant, says:

"Kandaka, take this gem and going back to where my father is, lay it reverently before him, to signify my heart's relation to him."

It is related that the gem mentioned was a beryl, which in the language of gems signifies purity and peace. It must be remembered that all Oriental languages give power to gems, perfumes and talismanic symbols. This fact makes direct translation of Oriental writings a difficult task for the Occidental scholar, who, until recently at least, gave no power to so-called "inanimate" things.

"And then for me request the king to stifle every fickle feeling of affection, and say that I, to escape from birth and age and death, have entered the forest of painful discipline.

"Not that I may get a heavenly birth, much less because I have no tenderness of heart, or that I cherish any cause of bitterness, but Only that I may escape this weight of sorrow; the accumulated long-night weight of covetous desire. I now desire to ease the load, so that it may be overthrown forever; therefore I seek the way of ultimate escape.

"If I should gain the way of emancipation, then shall I never need to put away my kindred, to leave my home, to sever ties of love. O grieve not for your son. The five desires of sense beget the sorrow; those held by lust themselves induce sorrow; my very ancestors, victorious kings, have handed down to me their kingly wealth; I, thinking only on eternal bliss, put it all away."

The meaning here conveyed is simple enough to understand. From a long line of ancestors who had ruled with the unquestioned authority of Oriental monarchs, the young prince felt that he had inherited much that would retard his soul's freedom. The examples of kings and emperors who have abandoned their possessions have been too few to cause us to believe that they have held these possessions as naught.

Through rivers of blood; through ages of despotism, and self-seeking, kings and emperors have maintained their vested rights bequeathing to their progeny the same desires; the same covetousness of worldly power; the same consideration for the lesser self; the same hypnotism that takes account of caste.

To escape from these fetters of the soul, into a realization of the Eternal Oneness of life, was no easy task for the inheritor of such desires and beliefs and appetites as an ancestry of rulers imposes.

And Prince Siddhartha was anxious to escape reincarnation—a theory or conviction inseparable from Oriental religion.

His reference to "fickle affection" means literally that selfish affection of the parent, which would retain the fleeting joy of a few short earthly years of companionship, while the larger and more perfect love would bid the child seek its birthright of godhood. The word "fickle" here would more properly be translated transitory.

Buddha's desire to escape from a continuous round of deaths and "leave-takings from kindred," does not necessarily imply an absorption into The Absolute; it may as logically be interpreted to mean, that liberation from the hypnotisms of externality (mukti) insures the possession and power of the gods—power over physical life and death, and this power need not mean a cessation from individual consciousness, but rather, a full realization of individual unity with the sum of all consciousness.

There is another mistaken interpretation of the means of attainment of that state of liberation, which has been alluded to in so many varied terms. The fact that Buddha, like many of the Oriental Masters, sought the seclusion of the forest; the isolation, and simplicity of the hermit,—has given rise to the belief, almost universally held among Oriental disciples, that liberation from maya, the delusions of the world, can not be attained save by these methods.

Monasteries are the result of this idea, and this Buddhistic practice was adopted by the first Christian church, since which time the real purpose and intention of the monastery and the nunnery have become lost in the concept of sacrifice or punishment. The Christian monk almost invariably retires to a monastery, not for the purpose of consciously attaining to that enlarged area of consciousness which insures liberation, mukti, but as an "outward and visible sign" that he is willing to undergo the sacrifice of worldly pleasures at the behest of the Lord Jesus. Thus, the real object of retirement is lost, and the sacrifice again becomes in the nature of a "bargain."

In the Bhagavad-Gita, we find these words:

"Renunciation and yoga by action both lead to the highest bliss; of the two, yoga by action is verily better than renunciation of action. He who is harmonized by yoga, the self-purified, self-ruled, the senses subdued, whose self is the self of all beings, although acting, yet is such an one not affected.

"He who acteth, placing all action in the eternal, abandoning attachment, is unaffected by sin as a lotus leaf by the waters."

This is interpreted according to the viewpoint of the translator, even as, among an audience of ten thousand persons, we may find almost as many interpretations, and shades of meaning of a musical composition.

True, the Oriental meaning seems to be the one that we shall cease to love friends, relatives, and lovers, abandoning them as one would abandon the furniture of one's household when outworn, and no longer of service.

We do not accept this interpretation.

To abandon one's friends, one's loved ones, yea, even one's would-be enemies is equivalent to leaving one's companions on a sinking raft and, without sentiment or remorse, save one's physical self from destruction.

No higher sentiment is known to struggling humanity than love of each other. "Greater love hath no man than this, that he lay down his life for a friend."

Oriental or Occidental philosophy, whichever may be presented to the mind, as an unfailing guide, should be distrusted, if that philosophy prescribes the abandonment of lover, friend, relative, neighbor, brother, companion. That is, if we accept the dictionary meaning of the word "abandoned" as translated into English.

A western avatar has said:

"I will not have what my brother can not," and in this we heartily concur, not hesitating to say that until all human life shall accept and realize the fullness of this message, we shall not, as a race, have attained to the inheritance that is ours.

But shall we then believe, that the Oriental doctrine is erroneous? Not necessarily.

Errors of interpretation are not only natural but inevitable, and this interpretation of abandonment is in line with the idea of sacrifice (using the word in its old sense of paying a debt), which prevailed throughout all the centuries just passed—centuries in which the idea of God was estimated by the conduct of the kings and monarchs of earth.

A later revelation or dispensation has given what the Illumined One said was a "new commandment," and it is one more in accord with our ideals of godhood.

"A new commandment I give unto you, that ye love one another."

But love, like everything which is, means much or little, according as the soul is advanced in knowledge, or is undeveloped.

Perfect and complete love is not selfish; it desires not possession, but union. There is a world of difference between the two words.

"The soul enchained is man, and free from chain is God," said Sri

Ramakrishna.

And the soul is enchained by illusion—by mistaking the effect for the cause, and by regarding the effect as the real, instead of realizing the incompleteness; the limitedness; the unsatisfying character of the changing—the external.

Not that the pursuit of the external is sinful, but it is unsatisfying, while the soul that has caught a glimpse of that wonderful ecstasy of Illumination, has found that which satisfies.

Upon this point of attainment of complete satisfaction, and certainty, all who have experienced the consciousness we are considering seem to agree, according to the testimony here submitted.

Chapter Five - Instances of Illumination and Its Effects

The term Illumination seems a fitting description of the state of consciousness which is frequently alluded to as cosmic consciousness. Without the light of understanding, which is a spiritual quality, words themselves are meaningless. When the mind becomes Illumined the spirit of the word is clear and where before the meaning was clouded, or perhaps altogether obscured, there comes to the Illumined One a depth of comprehension undreamed of by the merely sense-conscious person.

If we consider the recorded instances of Illumination found among Occidentals, we will find that such extreme intensity of effort as that which is reported of Sri Ramakrishna, and other Oriental sages, does not appear.

It would seem that the late Dr. Richard Maurice Bucke of Toronto, Canada, was the first in this country to present a specific classification of what he termed the "new" consciousness, and to describe in some detail, he experience of himself and others, notably Walt Whitman.

Dr. Bucke's first public exposition of these experiences was made at a congress of the British Medical Association in Montreal, Canada, in September of the year 1897. Dr. Bucke described this state of consciousness—a subject that seemed to him at that time to be a new one—in the following words:

"But of infinitely more importance than telepathy, and so-called spiritualism—no matter what explanation we give of these, or what their future is destined to be—is the final act here touched upon. This is, that superimposed upon self-consciousness as is that faculty upon simple consciousness, a third and higher form of consciousness is at present making its appearance in our race. This higher form of consciousness, when it appears, occurs as it must, at the full maturity of the individual, at or about the age of thirty-five, but almost always between the ages of thirty and forty. There have been occasional cases of it for the last two thousand years, and it is becoming more and more common. In fact, in all appearances, as far as observed, it obeys the laws to which every nascent faculty is subject. Many more or less perfect examples of this new faculty exist in the world to-day, and it has been my privilege to know personally and to have had the opportunity of studying, several men and women who have possessed it. In the course of a few more milleniums there should be born from the present human race, a higher type of man, possessing this higher type of consciousness. This new race, as it may well be called, would occupy toward us, a position such as that occupied by us toward the simple conscious 'alulus homo.' The advent of this higher, better and happier race, would simply justify the long agony of its birth through countless ages of our past. And it is the first article of my belief, some of the grounds for which I have endeavored to lay before you, that a new race is in course of evolution."

At a subsequent date, having given the subject further consideration and having collected data corroborative of his former observations, Dr. Bucke said:

"I have, in the last three years, collected twenty-three cases of this so-called cosmic consciousness. In each case the onset or incoming of the new faculty is always sudden, instantaneous. Among the unusual feelings the mind experiences, is a sudden sense of being immersed in flame or in a brilliant light. This occurs entirely without worrying or outward cause, and may happen at noonday or in the middle of the night, and the person at first feels that he is becoming insane.

"Along with these feelings comes a sense of immortality; not merely a feeling of certainty that there is a future life,—that would be a small matter—but a pronounced consciousness that the life now being lived is eternal, death being seen as a trivial incident which does not affect its continuity.

"Further, there is annihilation of the sense of sin, and an intellectual competency, not simply surpassing the old plane, but on an entirely new and higher plane. * * * The cosmic conscious race will not be the race that exists to-day, any more than the present is the same race that existed prior to the evolution of self-consciousness. A new race is being born from us, and this new race will in the near future, possess the earth."

Dr. Bucke later published an article in a current magazine, illustrating the illumination of his friend Walt Whitman, and supplemented with an account of his own experience. We quote briefly from Dr. Bucke's account of his own experience:

"I had spent the evening in a great city with some friends reading and discussing poetry and philosophy. We had occupied ourselves with Wordsworth, Shelley, Browning, and especially Whitman. We parted at midnight. I had a long drive in a hansom to my lodgings. My mind, deeply under the influence of the ideas, images and emotions called up by the reading and talk, was calm and peaceful. I was in a state of quiet, almost passive enjoyment, not actually thinking, but letting ideas, images and emotions flow of themselves, as it were, through my mind. All at once, without warning of any kind, I found myself wrapped in a flame-colored cloud. For an instant I thought of fire, an immense conflagration somewhere close by in that great city. The next moment I knew that the fire was within myself."

While Dr. Bucke is unquestionably right in his estimate of the fact that "a new race is being born," as he expresses it, there can scarcely be any question of individual age, in which the new consciousness may be expected. Physical maturity can have nothing whatever to do with the matter, since the acquisition of supra-consciousness is a matter of the maturity of the soul. This completement of the cycle of the soul's pilgrimage and service, may come at any age, as far as the physical body is concerned. Indeed, science records no definite age at which even physical maturity is invariably reached, although there is an approximate age.

A case recently widely commented upon was that of a child of six years who showed every symptom of senility or old age, which could hardly be possible without having passed what we call "maturity."

Again, we find that some persons retain every indication of youth, both of mind and body, long after their contemporaries have reached and passed middle age. It is coming more and more to be admitted that age is relative, and that what we know as the relative is the effect of mental operations. Mental operations are subject to change—to enlargement.

The advent of cosmic consciousness is, therefore, not subject to what we know as time, as applied to physical development.

Nor should we speak of cosmic consciousness as an acquisition, but rather as a realization, since the consciousness is, at all times. It always has been, it will always be. Our relation to it changes, as we develop from the sense conscious to the self-conscious state and finally to what we term the "cosmic" conscious state. This latter must of necessity have been as yet only imperfectly realized, even by those of the Illuminati, who are known to the world as avatars and saviours.

Several instances of the possession of cosmic consciousness by children, are personally known to the writer. A well-known woman writer in America thus describes a succession of experiences in what were evidently conditions of cosmic consciousness, although as she said, she did not until many years later realize what had taken place.

Like Lord Alfred Tennyson, who tells of inducing in himself a state of spiritual ecstasy or liberation, by repeatedly intoning his own name, this lady acquired the habit of repeating in wonder and awe the name by which she was called in the household, which was an abbreviation of her baptismal name. The effect is best described in her own words:

"It seems to me that I never could quite become accustomed to hear myself addressed by name. When some member of the household would call me from study or play—even at the early age of five or six years—I would instantly be seized with a feeling of great and almost overwhelming awe and amazement, at the sound, which I knew was in some way associated with me.

"I found it extremely difficult to identity myself with that name, and often when alone would repeat the name over and over, trying to find a solution of the 'why and wherefore.'

"At length this wonderment grew upon me to such an extent that I felt I must see this self of me that was called by a name.

"I acquired the habit of standing on a chair to gaze into the mirror above the chest of drawers in my mother's bed-room, and putting my face close to the mirror, I would gaze and gaze into the eyes I saw there, and repeat over and over the name which seemed to me not to belong to that 'other self' hidden behind those eyes. On one occasion I became quite entranced and fell from the chair, after which I refrained from looking into the mirror, although I did not for many years get over the feeling of wonderment at the sound of my own name, and many times, on repeating the name aloud, I would feel myself being lifted up into what seemed to me the clouds above my head, until I felt myself being 'melted,' as I termed it, into the moving cloud of soft transparent light.

"At this time I was between seven and eight years of age, and although I was far beyond children of my age, in my school studies, I was frequently admonished for being 'stupid,' owing to the fact that I could not remember the names of objects, nor could I be trusted on an errand.

"While walking from our house to the grocer's, scarcely a block away, I would feel that sudden wonderment and awe of my name steal over me, and again I would be transported to some unknown, yet immanent region, utterly losing consciousness of my surroundings. I would sometimes awake to find myself standing before the counter of the grocery store, struggling to remember who and where I was, and what it was that I had been sent to that strange place for."

This lady relates that she never dared to tell of her strange experiences, although she did not "outgrow" them until early womanhood, when she dropped the abbreviation of her name, and assumed her full baptismal name. Whether this latter fact had anything to do with the cessation of the experience is doubtful. At the same time, she declares that she can even now induce the same sensations, and transport herself into childhood again by repeating her childhood name.

The following extract from a paper published in London, England, in 1890, gives a description of an experience of a young man who had fallen into a condition which the physicians pronounced "catalepsy." This young man was at the time a medical student, and had always exhibited a tendency to entrancement, or catalepsy. On recovering from one of these cataleptic attacks, and being asked to give a description of his sensations or experiences, the young man said:

"I felt a kind of soothing slumber stealing over me. I became aware that I was floating in a vast ocean of light and joy. I was here, there, and everywhere. I was everybody and everybody was I. I knew I was I, and yet I knew that I was much more than myself. Indeed, it seemed to me that there was no division. That all the universe was in me and I in it, and yet nothing was lost or swallowed up. Everything was alive with a joy that would never diminish."

Such, in substance, was the attempt of this young man to describe what all who have experienced cosmic consciousness unite in saying is indescribable, for the very obvious reason that there are no words in which to express what is wordless, and inexpressible. This authentic account of a young man under twenty years of age, however, serves to prove that there is no special age of physical maturity in which the attainment of this state of consciousness may be expected.

This account was published seven years previous to Dr. Bucke's statement, and yet, since it is not quoted in Dr. Bucke's account, it is most unlikely that he had seen the article. Certainly the young man had never heard of the experience which Dr. Bucke later records, as "cosmic consciousness," and yet the similarity of the experience, with the many which have been recorded is almost startling.

The salient point in this account, as in most of the others which have found their way into public print, is the feeling of being in perfect harmony and union with everything in the universe. "I was everything and everything was I," said this young man, and again "I was here, there and everywhere at once," he says in an effort to describe something which in the very nature of it, must be indescribable in terms of sense consciousness.

Illustrative of the connection between religious ecstasy and cosmic consciousness, we find the experience of an illiterate negro woman, a celebrated religious and anti-slavery worker of the early part of the last century.

This woman was known as "Sojourner Truth" and was at least forty years of age in 1817, when she was given her freedom under a law which freed all slaves in New York state, who had attained the age of forty years.

Sojourner Truth never learned to read or write, and her education consisted almost entirely of that presentation of religious truth which finds its most successful converts in revivalism.

With this fact in mind, nothing less than the attainment of a wonderful degree of spiritual consciousness could account for her marvelous power of description, and her ready flow of language, when "exhorting."

Mrs. Harriet Beecher Stowe wrote of her, in an article published in the Atlantic Monthly, as early as 1863:

"I do not recollect ever to have been conversant with any one who had more of that silent and subtle power which we call personal presence, than this woman. In the modern spiritualistic phraseology, she would be described as having a 'strong sphere.'"

The wonderful mental endowment which seems to follow as a complement to the experience of Illumination, when not already present, as in the case of Whitman, for example, is characteristic of "Sojourner Truth," or Isabella, as she was baptized.

Naturally, this mental power, seemingly inconsistent with her humble origin, and her unlettered condition, is evidenced along those lines which made up the sum and substance of her life. Judging her from the broader concept of philosophy, Isabella appears somewhat fanatical, but the influence of her life and work was so great, that Wendell Phillips wrote of her:

"I once heard her describe the captain of a slave ship going up to judgment, followed by his victims as they gathered from the depths of the sea, in a strain that reminded me of Clarence's dream in Shakespeare, and equalled it. The anecdotes of her ready wit and quick striking replies are numberless. But the whole together give little idea of the rich, quaint, poetic and often profound speech of a most remarkable person, who used to say to us: 'You read books; God Himself talks to me.'"

Isabella's conviction that she had "talked to God," was unshakable, and was, indeed, the dynamic force which moved her. She was accustomed to tell of the strange and startling experience in which she met God face to face, and in which she said to Him: "Oh, God, I didn't know as you was so big." In the New England Magazine for March, 1901, there was given a full account of the work of this noted negro woman. Commenting on her sense of awe of the immensity of God "when she met him," the writer says:

"The consciousness of God's presence was like a fire around her and she was afraid, till she began to feel that somebody stood between her and this brilliant presence; and after a while she knew that this somebody loved her. At first, she thought it must be Cato, a preacher whom she knew or Deencia or Sally—people who had been her friends.

"We are not told whether these persons were living or dead, or whether she thought they had come in the flesh, or in the spirit to her relief. However this may be, she soon perceived that their images looked vile and black and could not be the beautiful presence that shielded her from the fires of God. She began to experiment with her inner vision, and found that when she said to the presence 'I know you, I know you,' she perceived a light; but when she said 'I don't know you,' the light went out.

"At last, she became aware that it was Jesus who was shielding her and loving her, and the world grew bright, her troubled thoughts were banished, and her heart was filled with praise and with love for all creatures. 'Lord, Lord,' she cried, 'I can love even de white folks.'"

The question will legitimately arise here, as to the authenticity of an experience in which Jesus is said to be personally guiding and shielding her, but it must be remembered that the mind is the medium through which the spiritual realization must be expressed and, as has been stated previously, the description of the phenomenon of Illumination, particularly when experienced in a sudden influx must partake of the character of the mind of the illumined one.

William James, late professor of Psychology of Harvard University, in his exhaustive book The Varieties of Religious Experiences, in the chapter on "The Value of Saintliness," says:

"Now in the matter of intellectual standards, we must bear in mind that it is unfair, where we find narrowness of mind, always to impute it as a vice to the individual for in religious and theological matters, he probably absorbs his narrowness from his generation. Moreover, we must not confound the essentials of saintliness with its accidents, which are the special determination of these passions at any historical moment. In these determinations the saints will usually be loyal to the temporary idols of their tribe."

Applying this explanation to the case of "Sojourner Truth," we may realize that the literal conception of Jesus as her guide and shield, was a mental image, inevitable with her, as Jesus was the motive power of her every thought and act. And although at the moment of her Illumination, she realized the "bigness" of God, later, in arranging and recording the phenomenon, in her mental note-book, she tabulated it with all she knew of God—the religious enthusiasm of her work of conversion to the religion of Jesus.

Says James, commenting upon the question of conversion in human experience: and this tendency to what seems a narrow and limited viewpoint:

"If you open the chapter on 'Association,' of any treatise on Psychology, you will read that a man's ideas, aims and objects form diverse internal groups, and systems, relatively independent of one another. Each 'aim' which he follows awakens a certain specific kind of interested excitement, and gathers a certain group of ideas together in subordination to it as its associates."

It is perhaps natural to assume that most instances of the attainment of Illumination, have been inseparable from religious devotion, or at least contemplative mysticism. This view is held almost exclusively by Orientals, and seems to have been shared to a great extent by western commentators upon the subject.

A notable example among Occidentals, bearing the religious aspect, and one which is important from the fact that the person detailing his experience, was a man of mental training, is the case of Rev. Charles G. Finney, formerly president of Oberlin College.

In his "Memoirs," Dr. Finney describes what Orthodox Christians generally call the "baptism of the Holy Spirit":

"I had retired to a back room for prayer," writes Dr. Finney, "and there was no fire or light in the room; nevertheless it appeared to me as if it were perfectly light. As I went in and shut the door after me, it seemed as if I met the Lord Jesus Christ face to face. It did not occur to me then nor did it for some time afterwards, that it was wholly a mental state.

"On the contrary, it seemed to me a reality, that he stood before me and I fell down at his feet and poured out my soul to him. I wept aloud like a child and made such confessions as I could with choked utterance.

"It seemed to me that I bathed his feet with my tears, and yet I had no distinct impression that I touched him, that I recollect. As I turned and was about to take my seat, I received a mighty baptism of the Holy Ghost.

"Without any expectation, without even having the thought in my mind, that there was any such thing for me, without any recollection that I had ever heard the thing mentioned, by any person in the world, the Holy Spirit descended upon me in a manner that seemed to go through me body and soul.

"I could feel the impression like the waves of electricity going through me and through me. Indeed, it seemed to come in waves of liquid love. For I could not express it in any other way. It seemed like the very breath of God. I can recollect distinctly that it seemed to fan me like immense wings. No words can express the wonderful love that was shed abroad in my heart.

"I wept aloud with joy and love. These waves came over me, and over me, one after the other, until I recollect that I cried out, 'I shall die if these waves continue to pass over me.' I said 'Lord, I cannot bear any more.'"

We will note, that although Dr. Finney says that he could not remember ever having heard the thing mentioned by any person, yet he felt "the baptism of the Holy Spirit." It is practically impossible that Dr. Finney could have lived in an age and a community which was essentially strict in its Orthodoxy, without having heard of the phrase "baptism of the Holy Spirit," even though the words had escaped his immediate recollection. However, the point that characterizes Dr. Finney's experience, in common with all others, is that of seeing an intense light, and of the realization of the overwhelming force of love.

The relation of this experience to a creed or system of religion, is something which, we believe, may be accounted for, as Professor James has said, on the fact of "historical determination."

Until very recently, the idea that spirituality was impossible save in connection with religious systems, and rigid discipline, has been quite general.

In the case of Dr. Finney, we find that all his life previous to this experience he had been noted for his simplicity and child-like trust. Following his Illumination we learn that he became a man of great influence, and power, because of "the wonderful humanity which he radiated."

Similar in experience, in its effects, is a case related by Theodore F. Seward, the well-known American philanthropist, Mr. Seward relates the following story:

"The strange experience which I here relate came to a friend whom I knew intimately, and from whose lips I received the account. It is a lady in middle life, who has for years been an earnest seeker for truth and spiritual light. She was alone in her room sewing.

"Thinking, as was her wont, of spiritual things and feeling a strong sense of the presence and power of God, she suddenly had a consciousness of being surrounded by a brilliant white light, which seemed to radiate from her person. The light continued for some minutes, and at the same time, she felt a great spiritual uplifting and an enlargement of her mental powers, as if the limitations of the body were transcended, and her soul's capacities were in a measure set free for the moment. The experience was unique, above and beyond the ordinary current of human life, and while the vision or impression passed away, a permanent effect was produced upon her mind. She had never heard the term 'cosmic consciousness,' and did not know that the subject it covers is beginning to be discussed."

It must be noted that in these experiences, the idea most strongly felt was the one of the "power and presence of God," and we are impressed with the fact that, no matter how varied may be the creeds of the world, as founded by "saviours" and incarnations of God, there is a unity among all races, as to the fact of a one supreme universal power, which is Aum, the Absolute, and which must represent perfect love and perfect peace, since all who have glimpsed their unity with this power, testify to a feeling of happiness, peace and satisfaction, rare and exalted.

By comparing the experience of those who have attained this state of liberation from illusion, through religious rites and ceremonies, or "sacrifice to God," as it is not infrequently called, with the experience of those who have recorded the phenomenon, apparently arriving at the goal through intellectual and moral aspiration, we will find that the results are almost identical, and the after-effects similar.

It has been said that those who attain liberation have invariably sought to found a new system of worship, and this fact has given rise to the many paths or methods of attainment which have been taught by various Illumined Ones, both in the Orient and in the western world, supplementary as it were to the main great religious systems.

We will take a short survey of a few of these systems in Japan and India in comparatively modern times, or at least during the last two thousand years, which is modern compared to the history of the Orient.

Chapter Six - Examples of Cosmic Consciousness, Who Have Founded New Systems of Religion

The early religion of Japan, before the advent of Buddhism, was extremely simple.

It consists of the postulate that there was but one God, Kami, from him all things came, and to him all things shall return. As has been stated previously, the chief injunction of Shintoism is: "Keep your body and your mind clean, and trust Kami."

Shintoism literally translated, means "the way to God," and includes the belief that all persons ultimately reach the place where God dwells, and become "one with Him."

In present day interpretations and descriptions of Shintoism, we read of the "heathen" belief that Kami himself dwells in person, in the "inner temple" or sacred place of Shinto temples.

This idea doubtless exists as a reality among the very ignorant superstitious devotees, much as among the ignorant Catholics we find the unquestioned belief that the actual body and blood of Jesus the Christ is contained in the Eucharist.

The Shinto temple always contains an "inner or sacred shrine," which is equivalent to the "holy of holies," of the Mystic Brotherhoods, and typifies the fact that within and not without, will be found the God in man, by finding which, man reaches liberation, or cessation from the cycle of births and deaths.

A Shinto funeral is an occasion for rejoicing, because the departed one may be a step farther on the way to God, and since his ancestors were directly responsible, as a favor, for his occasion to become reborn, thus fulfilling the law of karma, the Shintoist pays much respect to his ancestors.

The advent of Buddhism into Japan was made possible by the simple fact that the people were becoming somewhat disgruntled with Shintoism, because of its emphasis upon the never-to-be questioned postulate that the Mikado and his progeny was the direct gift of Kami to his people, to be obeyed without demur, and to be adored as divine.

Several generations of Mikados who did not fulfil the ideal of Deity—an ideal to which even savages attach the qualities of justice and mercy—left the masses ready and eager to grasp at a religion that gave them some other personified god, than the Mikado, much as a drowning man clutches at a straw.

The Lord Buddha was a prince, therefore worship of him would not be an absolutely impossible step—an unforgivable breach of contract with the Mikado, and as he exhibited the qualities of humility and mercy and tolerance, he was welcomed. The religion of Japan is to-day regarded as Buddhistic, although the Imperial family, and consequently the army and the navy are to all outward appearance, Shintoists.

Coming, then, to a consideration of the varying sects of Buddhism in Japan, and the corresponding sects in India, we find that there have been nine different incarnations of God, and that another, and, it is believed the final one, is expected.

The intelligent and open minded seeker after truth of whatever race or color, will find in the instructions given man by each and every great teacher, whether we believe in them as especially "divine" or as mere humans who have attained to the realization of their godhood (avatars,) a complete unity of purpose, and if these teachers differ in method of attainment, it is only because of the immutable fact that there can be no one and only way of attainment.

Methods and systems are established consistently with the age and character of those whom they are designed to assist in finding the way.

And again we must emphasize the fact that by the phrase "the way," we mean the way to a realization of the godhood within the inner temple of man's threefold nature.

Thus, the intelligent, unprejudiced student of the religions and philosophies of all times and all races, will find that, while there are many and diverse paths to the goal of "salvation," the goal itself means unity with the Causeless Cause, wherein exists perfection.

Perhaps it has been left for the expected Incarnate God, which Christians speak of as "the second coming of Christ," to make clear the problem as to whether this attainment or completement means an absorption of individual consciousness, or whether it will be an adding to the present incarnation, of the memory of past lives, in such a manner that no consciousness shall be lost, but all shall be found.

In considering instances of cosmic consciousness, mukti, which have been recorded as distinctly religious experiences, and the effect of this attainment, the system best known to the Occident, is contained in the philosophy of Vedanta, expounded and interpreted to western understanding by the late Swami Vivekananda.

But it should be understood that the philosophy taught by Vivekananda is not strictly orthodox Hinduism. It bears the same relation to the old religious systems of India that Unitarianism bears to orthodox Christianity such as we find in Catholicism, and its off-shoots.

Vivekananda honored and revered and followed, according to his interpretation of the message, Sri Ramakrishna, whom an increasing number of Hindus regard as the latest incarnation of Aum—the Absolute. Not that the reader is to understand, that Sri Ramakrishna's message contradicted the essential character of the basic principles of orthodox Hinduism, as set down in the Vedas and the Upanashads.

The same difference of emphasis upon certain points, or interpretations of meaning exists in the Orient, as in the western world, in regard to the possible meaning of the Scriptures.

Sri Ramakrishna, who passed from this earth life at Cossipore, in 1886, was a disciple of the Vedanta system, as founded by Vyasa, or by Badarayana, authorities failing to agree as to which of these traditional sages of India founded the Vedantic system of religion or philosophy.

Vedanta, particularly as interpreted by Sri Ramakrishna and his successors, offers a wider field of effort, and a more intellectual consideration of Hindu religion than that of the Yoga system as interpreted from the original Sankhya system by Patanjali, about 300 B.C.

Patanjali's sutras are considered the most complete system of Yoga practice, for the purpose of mental control, and psychic development. Patanjali's sutras are almost identical with those employed in the Zen sect of Buddhist monasteries, throughout Japan.

These sutras, together with Buddhist mantrams will be considered in a subsequent chapter, devoted to the development of spiritual consciousness as taught by the Oriental sages and philosophers.

One other great teacher of modern times who has left a large following, was Lord Gauranga, who was born in India in the early part of the fifteenth century. Gauranga was worshipped as the Lord God, whether with his consent, or without, it is not exactly clear, even though his biographers are united on the fact of his divine origin.

Those who have espoused the message of Gauranga claim that he brought to the world "a beautiful religion, such as had never before been known." But, as this claim is made for all teachers and founders of religions and philosophies, we suggest that the reader compare the message of Lord Gauranga with those of other avatars and teachers.

Lord Gauranga's message is known as Vaishnavitism, and we will here consider only those passages of his doctrine which shed light upon his attainment of cosmic consciousness. Certainly his breadth of mind, and his standards of tolerance, justice and consideration for all other systems of worship, would indicate his claim to cosmic consciousness.

One of the contentions of the Vaishnavas is that they alone of all religious faiths, admit the divine birth and mission of the founders of all religions.

Thus the Christians have declared that Jesus was the only Son of God; the Buddhists have claimed Buddha; the Hebrews have clung tenaciously to their prophets as the only true messengers from heaven, and the Mohammedans have refused, until the present century, to even sit at the table with the "infidels" who would not acknowledge Mohammed as the only true incarnation of Allah.

It is well to remember that these claims have been made by the blind followers of these great teachers, and that it is almost certain that not any one of them made such claim for himself. Certainly he did not, if he had attained to spiritual consciousness.

One passage from the doctrines of Gauranga is almost identical with many others who have sought to express the feeling of security, of deathlessness which comes to the soul which has realized cosmic consciousness. He says:

"My Beloved, whether you clasp me unto your heart, or you crush me by that embrace, it is all the same to me. For you are no other than my own, the sole partner of my soul."

The gospel of Gauranga and his followers is, indeed, much more a gospel of love, than of methods of worship, or of intellectual research.

The realization of our union with God, in deathless love, is the key-note of the message, and this great joy or bliss comes to the soul as soon as it has attained Illumination through love.

God is alluded to in Vaishnavism most frequently as Anandamaya— meaning all joy. Vaishnavism more nearly resembles the gospel of Jesus, as taught by orthodoxy, than it does the Vedantic systems, since it does, not claim that God is within each human organism, as the seed is within the fruit, but that, by love, we may gain heaven or the state or place where God dwells.

"If you would worship God, as the Giver of Bounties, then shall the prayer be answered, and further connection cut off, God having answered the demand. So if you would worship God in simple love, He will send love. The real devotee seeks to establish a relationship with God which will endure. He will ask only to worship and love God, and pray that his soul may cling to God in divine reverence and love." Thus, say the Vaishnavas, "God serves as he is served, in absolute justice."

Another salient point which the followers of Lord Gauranga emphasize, is the "All-Sweetness" of God. This idea is impressed, doubtless that the devotee may not feel an impossible barrier between himself and so great and all-powerful a being, as God, when His Omnipotence is considered. The idea is similar to that of the Roman church, which bids its untutored children to select some patron saint, or to say prayers to the Virgin Mary, because these characters were once human and seem to be nearer, and more approachable than the Great God whose Majesty and All-Mightiness have been exploited.

Be that as it may, the fact remains, that Lord Gauranga is said to have earned the devotion and love of some of the most learned pundits of India and, according to a recent biographer, "he had all the frailties of a man; he ate and slept like a man. In short, he behaved generally like an ordinary human being, but yet he succeeded in extorting from the foremost sages of India, the worship and reverence due a God."

The fact that Lord Gauranga "behaved like a man," is comforting, to say the least, and presages the coming of a day when "behaving like a man" will not be considered ungodly. When that time shall have arrived, surely there will be less mysticism of the hysterical variety and probably fewer hypocrites.

Very unlike Lord Gauranga, is the report of a writer of India, who tells of the effects of cosmic consciousness upon Tukaram, considered to be one of the greatest saints and poets of Ancient India. Tukaram lived early in the sixteenth century, some years later than Lord Gauranga.

This Maharashtra saint is chiefly remembered for his beautiful description of the effects of Illumination, in which he likens the human soul to the bride, and the bridegroom is God. This poem is called "Love's Lament," and might have been written by an impassioned lover to his promised bride.

The life of Tukaram, like that of the late Sri Ramakrishna Paramanansa, was one long agony of yearning and struggle for that peace of soul which he craved. One of his chroniclers thus describes, in brief, the final struggle and the subsequent attainment of Illumination of this good man:

"Selfless, he sought to gather no crowds of idle admiring disciples about him, but followed what his conscience dictated. He listened not to the counsel of his relatives and friends, who thought he had gone mad; and he bore in patience the well-meant but harsh rebukes of his second wife. After a long mental struggle, the agonies of which he has recorded in heart-rending words, now entreating God in the tenderest of terms, now resigning himself to despair, now appealing with the petulance of a pet child for what he deemed his birthright, now apologizing in all humility for thus taking liberties with his Mother-God, he succeeded at last in gaining a restful place of beatitude—a state in which he merged his soul in the universal soul,"—that is, Illumination, or cosmic consciousness.

Sadasiva Brahman, one of the great Siddhas, and a comparatively modern sage of India, left a Sanskrit poem called Atmavidyavilasa, which gives a comprehensive description of the experience and the effects of Illumination, as for example:

"The sage whose mind by the grace of his blessed Guru is merged in his own true nature (Existence, Intelligence, and Bliss Absolute), that great Illumined one, wise, with all egotism suppressed, and extremely delighted within himself, sports in joy."

"He who is himself alone, who has known the secret of bliss, who has firmly embraced peace, who is magnanimous and whose feelings other than those of the atman, have been allayed, that person sports on his pleasant couch of self-bliss."

"The pure moon of the prince of recluses, who is fit to be worshipped by gods and whose moonlight of intelligence that dispels the darkness of ignorance causes the lily of the earth to blossom, shines forth in the abode of the all-pervading Essence of Light."

The above stanzas represent a more impersonal idea of the bliss of attainment than those of many others who have experienced Illumination, but they emphasize the same point that we find throughout all writings of the Illuminati, namely, the realization of the kingdom within, rather than without, and the necessity of selflessness—meaning the subjugation of the lesser self, the mental, to the soul.

We come now to a consideration of the life and character of the Lord Buddha, whose influence is still stronger in all parts of the world than that of any other person who has ever taught the precepts of attainment.

In Japan, for example, Buddhism, in its various branches, or interpretations, is the religion of the vast majority and even where Shintoism is the method of worship, the influence of Buddhism may be seen. So too, we find in Japan, a form of Buddhism, which shows evidences of the influence of Shintoism, but I think it may be admitted that Japan, above all other countries, represents to-day, the religion of Buddhism.

Buddhism has been called the "religion of enlightenment," but the term "illumination" as it is used to describe the attainment of cosmic consciousness, is what is meant, rather than the purely intellectual quality which we are accustomed to think of as enlightenment.

Sakyamuni, another name for Buddhism, means also illumination, or realization of the saving character of the light within.

The lamp is the most important symbol in, Buddhism, as it typifies the divine flame or illumination (which is cosmic consciousness), as the goal of the disciple.

Another interpretation of the symbol of the lamp, is that of the power of the lamp to shed its rays to light the way of those who are traveling "in the gloom," and by so doing, it lights the flame of illumination in others, without diminishing its own power. An article of faith reads:

"As one holds out a lamp in the darkness that those who have eyes may see the objects, even so has the doctrine been made clear by the Lord in manifold exposition."

Again, in the Book of the Great Decease, we learn that Buddha admonished his disciples to "dwell as lamps unto yourselves." Another symbol used throughout Japan as a means of teaching the masses the essential doctrines of "The Compassionate One," has become familiar to occidental people as a sort of "curio." It is that of the three monkeys carved in wood or ivory.

One monkey is covering his eyes with both paws; another has stopped his ears; and the third has his paw pressed tightly over his mouth. The lesson briefly told is to "see no evil; hear no evil; speak no evil," and the reason that the monkey is employed as the symbol, is because the monkey, more than any other animal, resembles primitive man. If, then, we would rise from the monkey, or animal condition (the physical or animal part of the human organism), we must avoid a karma of consciousness of evil.

Buddhism is full of symbolism, and these symbols must be interpreted according to the age, or of the individual consciousness of the interpreter, or the translator. But the fundamental doctrine of Buddha is essentially one of renunciation as applied to the things of the world. Nevertheless this quality of renunciation has been greatly exaggerated during the centuries, because of the fact that the Lord Buddha had so much to give up, viewed from the standpoint of worldly ethics.

In the following "sayings of Buddha," we find that the quest of the noble sage was for that supraconsciousness wherein change and decay were not, rather than that he regarded the things of the senses, as sinful. For example:

"It is not that I am careless about beauty, or am ignorant of human joys; but only that I see on all the impress of change; therefore, my heart is sad and heavy." Or this:

"A hollow compliance and a protesting heart, such method is not for me to follow: I now will seek a noble law, unlike the worldly methods known to men. I will oppose disease, and change and death, and strive against the mischief wrought by these, on men."

According to the Samyutta Nikaya, the twelve Nidanas (or chain of consequences) are:

"On ignorance depends karma;
"On karma depends consciousness;
"On consciousness depends name and form;
"On name and form depends the six organs of sense."
"On contact depends sensation;
"On sensation depends desire;
"On desire depends attachment;
"On attachment depends existence;
"On existence depends birth;
"On birth depend old age and death, sorrow, lamentation, misery, grief, and despair.

"Thus does this entire aggregation of misery arise."

Having arrived at this conclusion, the problem may be solved by learning how to avoid existence. But, let us consider what the term "existence" means. The common acceptance of the word, as used in the English, seems to include being; but if we will consider the word in its literal meaning, when analyzed, we find that it comes from "est" (to be), and the prefix "ex," meaning actually "not-being."

The word Being, is a synonym for eternal life—for Deity. It does not savor of anything that has been created, or that will terminate. Being is, therefore, to cease to ex-ist, is to cease to live under the spell of the illusory and changing quality of maya, or externality.

Far from meaning to be "wiped out," or absorbed into The Absolute, in the sense of complete loss of consciousness, it means the eternal retention of consciousness, unhampered by the delusion of sense as a reality.

To escape from this chain of illusory ideas, and their consequences, the obvious necessity is to claim the soul's right to Being. This is done by dispelling ignorance (A-vidya) by vidya (knowledge). Thus karma ceases:

"On the cessation of karma ceases consciousness of self;
"On the cessation of this consciousness of self, cease name and form;
"On the cessation of name and form, cease the organs of sense;
"On the cessation of sense, ceases contact;
"On the cessation of contact, ceases sensation;
"On the cessation of sensation, ceases desire;
"On the cessation of desire ceases attachment;
"On the cessation of attachment ceases existence;
"On the cessation of existence, ceases birth.

"On the cessation of birth cease old age, and death; sorrow; lamentation; misery; grief and despair. Thus does the entire aggregation of misery cease."

But, as to the exact interpretation of all these, Buddha himself says:

"Ye must rely upon the truth; this is your highest, strongest vantage ground; the foolish masters practicing superficial wisdom, grasp not the meaning of the truth; but to receive the law, not skillfully to handle words and sentences, the meaning then is hard to know, as in the night-time, if traveling and seeking for a house, if all be dark within, how difficult to find."

But let it be understood, that Buddhism as now taught and practiced is necessarily colored by the effect of the centuries which have elapsed since the Lord Buddha lived and taught the precepts of his Illumination. Modern Buddhism, as a religious system of worship bears the same relation to Prince Siddhartha, as does modern Christianity to Jesus of Nazareth.

A short review of the life and character of the personalities around whom the great religious systems of the world have been formed will aid us in perceiving the unity of thought and character of the Illumined, and the similarity of reports as to the effect of this realization of cosmic consciousness will be apparent.

Chapter Seven - Moses, The Law-Giver

The salient feature of the law as given by Moses unto his people, the Jews, is that of strict cleanliness of mind and body. In this we find a similarity to the oft-repeated behest of Gautama, the Buddha, who constantly admonished his followers to keep their hearts pure and their minds and bodies clean.

This spirit of cleanliness finds also a counterpart in the saying ascribed to Jesus, "blessed are the pure in heart."

The cleanliness here referred to is doubtless not so much physical neatness as mental purity of thought—thought free from doubt and calumny and petty deceits and hypocrisy and selfishness and debasing perversions of the life forces; but during various stages of history we find that all teachings have their esoteric and their exoteric application.

The law, as enunciated by Moses, according to the Jewish reports, laid much stress upon physical cleanliness, as an attribute of godhood.

But Moses, if we may credit reports, was something far more inspired and illumined than a mere physical culturist—commendable as is personal cleanliness—and his admonitions were the result of that fine sense of discrimination and enlightenment which comes from cosmic perception even if he had not experienced the deeper, fuller realization of liberation, of which Buddha is a shining example.

It is evident that the laws laid down by Moses were taught and practised by the Egyptians many many years prior to the time in which Moses lived, which from the most reliable authorities, must have been about four to five hundred years before the Exodus.

This does not detract from the evidence that the great Egyptian-Hebrew, was a man of wonderful intellectual attainments, and from what we know of modern examples of Illumination, he also possessed a degree of cosmic consciousness.

The story of the seemingly miraculous birth of Moses, and the mystery with which his ancestry is surrounded, is also typical of one who has attained to cosmic consciousness.

The Illumined one realizes his birthlessness and his deathlessness, and expresses it in symbolism, meaning of course, the realization that as the spirit is never born and can never die, the idea of age is an unreality—and should find no place in the consciousness of one who regards himself as an indestructible atom of the Cosmos.

But the evidences regarding the probable Illumination of Moses are to be found in the reports of his ascension of Mt. Sinai, and what occurred there.

The phenomenon of the great light which is inseparable from instances of cosmic consciousness, and which gives to the phenomenon its name "Illumination," was apparently marked in the case of Moses.

The "burning bush," which he describes is the experience of the mind when the illusion of sense has ceased, even temporarily, to obscure the mental vision.

"And the angel of the Lord appeared unto him in a flame of fire, and out of the midst of a bush; and he looked and behold, the bush burned with fire and the bush was not consumed."

There is a subtler interpretation to this report than that usually given, even by those who realize that this expression is an evidence of the sudden influx of supra consciousness which attends the soul's liberation from the limits of sense consciousness.

The "burning bush" is synonymous with the "tree of life" which is ever alive with the "fires of creation."

All who realize liberation are endowed with the power to understand this symbol. For those who have not attained to this degree of consciousness, the esoteric meaning is necessarily hidden.

The phenomenon of the strange mystical light which seems to enfold and bathe the Illumined one, is concisely expressed in the case of Moses.

"And it came to pass, that when Moses came down from Mount Sinai with the tablets of the testimony in hand, that Moses wist not that the skin of his face shone, or sent forth beams by reason of his speaking with Him.

"And when Aaron and all the children of Israel saw Moses behold! the skin of his face shone and they were afraid to come nigh him."

Again we find in the case of Moses, a momentary fear of the phenomenon which he was experiencing, in the influx of light and the sound of the voice which seems to accompany the light.

The interpretation given the words spoken, and the identity of the voice is ever dependent upon the time and character of the mind experiencing the Illumination.

Thus Moses claims to have heard the voice of the God of the Hebrews, but the probabilities are, that the "voice" is the mental operations of the person experiencing the phenomenon of supra-consciousness, and this interpretation will vary with what Professor James calls the "historical determination," i.e. it is dependent upon the age in which the illumined one lived, and upon the character of the impressions previously absorbed.

This apparent difference of report, as to the identity of the "voice," is of small import.

The salient point is that each person relating his experience has heard a voice giving more or less explicit instructions and promises.

In each instance it has been characterized as the voice of the God of their desire, and adoration.

Certainly, whatever may be our opinions as to whether God, as we understand the term, talked to Moses, giving him such explicit commands as the great leader afterwards laid down to his people accompanied by the insurmountable barrier to dissent or discussion, "thus saith the Lord," we can but admit that the prophet was possessed of intellectual power far in advance of his time, and his laws did indeed, save his people from self destruction, through uncleanliness and strife, and dense ignorance.

The ten commandments have been the "word of God" to all men for lo! these many ages, and even Jesus could but add one other commandment to those already in use: "Another commandment give I unto you—that ye love one another."

To sum up the evidences of cosmic consciousness, or Illumination, as reported in the case of Moses, we find:

The experience of great light as seen on Horeb.
The "voice" which he calls the voice of "The Lord."
The sudden and momentary fear, and humility.
The shining of his face and form, as though bathed in light.
The subsequent intellectual superiority over those of his time.
The perfect assurance and confidence of authority and "salvation."
The desire for solitude, which caused him to die alone in the vale of Moab.
The intense desire to uplift his people to a higher consciousness.

Chapter Eight - Gautama—The Compassionate

Gautama, prince of the house of Siddhartha, of the Sakya class, was born in northern India in the township of Kapilavastu, in the year 556 B.C., according to the best authorities, as interpreted and reported by Max Muller.

The Japanese tradition agrees with this, practically, stating that O Shaka Sama (signifying one born of wisdom and love) was born as a Kotai Si, crown prince of the Maghada country.

We have the assurance that as a youth, Gautama, like Jesus, exhibited a serious mindedness and an insight into matters spiritual, which astonished and dumbfounded his hearers, and the sages who gave him respectful attention.

Some accounts even go so far as to state that at the very moment of his birth the young prince was able to speak, and that his words ascended "even to the gods of the uppermost Brahma-world."

Divesting the traditions that surround the birth and early life of the world's great masters, of much that has been interpolated by a designing priesthood, we may yet conclude that a certain seriousness, and a deep sympathy with the sorrows of their fellowmen, would naturally characterize these inspired ones, even while they were still in their early youth.

It is evident that the young Prince Siddhartha was subject to meditation and that these meditations led at times to complete trance.

It is reported that one day while out riding in all the pomp and accoutrements of the son of a ruling king, he was visited by an angel (a messenger from the gods of Devachan), and told that if he would lessen the sorrows of the world that he must renounce his right to his father's kingdom and go into the jungle, becoming a hermit, and devoting his life to fasting, prayer and meditation, in order to fit himself for the work of preaching the "way of liberation," which consisted of, first of all, to take no life; be pure in mind; be as the humblest, which latter admonition found little favor with the world of his personal environment where caste was and still is, a seemingly ineradicable race-thought.

The sorrows of humanity weighed heavily upon his heart, and the superficialities of the wealthy and ostentatious court in which he lived, irked his outspoken and truth-loving spirit.

Surrounded, as he was, by wealth and ease, with time for contemplation and a mind given to philosophic speculation, the young prince found no sense of comfort or permanent satisfaction in his own immunity from want and sorrow. He pondered long upon the way to become freed from the "successive round of births and deaths," and thus pondering, he sought solitude in which to find his questions answered.

Fasting and penance have ever been the gist of the instruction given to those who would "find the way to God," and so to this end Gautama fasted and prayed, and practised self-sacrifice.

But the attainment of liberation was not easy, and Siddhartha suffered long and practiced self-mortification assiduously, at length being rewarded; and "there arose within him the eye to perceive the great and noble truths which had been handed down; the knowledge of their nature; the understanding of their cause; the wisdom that lights the true path; the light that expels darkness."

The terrible struggle which characterized the attainment of cosmic consciousness, by so many of the sages and saviours of history, is, we believe, clue to the fact that no one individual may hope to rise so immeasurably above the plane of the race-consciousness of his day and age, except through intense and overwhelming desire.

Gautama abandoned his heritage, his relatives, his wife to whom he was devoted, and his infant son, as we have previously stated, not because Illumination is purchasable at so terrible a price, but because his desire to know transcended all other desires, and in order to be free from the demands made upon him, he must of necessity, seek solitude.

Few examples of the attainment of cosmic consciousness are as complete and of such fullness, as that attained by Buddha, and no instance which history affords has left so great an effect upon the world.

It is estimated that at least one-third of the human race are Buddhists. This is not saying that any such number of persons are like unto Buddha, nor do we contend that this is any evidence that his message is greater or more fraught with truth than that of other illumined ones.

The intelligent student of occultism in all its phases will arrive, sooner or later, at the inevitable conclusion that all illumined souls have seen and have taught the same fundamental truth.

Buddha was convinced that in The Absolute, or First Cause, there could be no sin and consequently no sorrow, and he persistently sought to inaugurate such systems of conduct and such a standard of morals as would lead the disciple back to godhood, or liberation from the "wheel of causation."

To keep the mind pure and clean was the burden of his cry, well knowing that the mind is the fertile field wherein illusions of sense consciousness thrive. He says:

"Mind is the root (of evil); actions proceed from the mind. If anyone speak or act from a corrupt mind, suffering will follow, as the dust follows the rolling wheel."

That we can not expect to escape the result of our thoughts and acts was ever a doctrine of Buddha, albeit, he seems also to have sought to make clear to his disciples, the UNREALITY of sin as a part of the indestructible "First Cause."

Many Buddhist sects interpret the doctrines of Buddha to deny a belief in a future existence, in at least as far as identity is concerned, but this conception is not consistent with the most reliable reports, neither is it in keeping with the extreme peace and satisfaction which all illumined ones experience.

If extinction of identity were the goal of Illumination, it is inconceivable that the illumined ones should report the attainment of perfect satisfaction and bliss.

Besides, it is clearly stated that Gautama told his disciples that he had already entered Nirvana, while yet in the body.

"My mind is free from passions; is released from the follies of the world.

I have gained the victory," said Lord Buddha to his disciple Ananda.

It is also asserted that Buddha appeared in his own "glorified body" to his disciples after his physical dissolution, plainly indicating that far from being swallowed up in The Absolute, he had acquired godhood in his present body.

Detailing the advantages of a pure life, Buddha said to his disciples:

"The virtuous man rejoices in this world, and he will rejoice in the next; in both worlds has he joy. He rejoices, he exults, seeing the purity of his deed."

Again, alluding to a sage (rahan), Buddha is reported to have said:

"He is indeed blest, having conquered all his passions, and attained the state of Nirvana."

This alluded to the acquisition of Nirvana while still in the physical body. In other words, as we of this century understand the teaching, he had experienced cosmic consciousness.

The modern version of the commandments of Buddha are almost identical with those of the Christian creed, and these commandments are, as we have previously observed, the same that Moses laid down for the guidance of his people. That they were old before Moses was born, is also more than problematical.

It is also more than probable that Buddha did not personally write the ethical code which we now find submitted as the "Commandments of Buddha," but that Buddha merely emphasized them.

These commandments are not, however, understood, by the intelligent Buddhist as "sacred," in the sense that "God spoke unto Buddha."

Moses doubtless assumed to have been divinely instructed in the law, although that supposition may be erroneous. He may have had in mind the same fundamental idea which all those expressing cosmic consciousness have had, that of being a mouthpiece of a higher power, rather than to attract to themselves any adulation or worship, as being specially divine.

The "Commandments," therefore, as translated and ascribed to modern Buddhism, are an ethical and moral code for the MORTAL consciousness, rather than a formula for developing cosmic consciousness. These commandments are:

1—Thou shalt kill no animal whatever, from the meanest insect up to man.
2—Thou shalt not steal.
3—Thou shalt not violate the wife of another.
4—Thou shalt speak no word that is false.
5—Thou shalt not drink wine, nor anything that may intoxicate.
6—Thou shalt avoid all anger, hatred and bitter language.
7—Thou shalt not indulge in idle and vain talk, but shall do all for others.
8—Thou shalt not covet thy neighbor's goods.
9—Thou shalt not harbor envy, nor pride, nor revenge, nor malice, nor the desire of thy neighbor's death or misfortune.
10—Thou shalt not follow the doctrines of false gods.

And the devotee is assured, even as in the Christian creed, that "he who keeps these commandments, shall enter Nirvana—the rest of Buddha." But let it be understood that Gautama, the Lord Buddha, did not formulate these commandments. Neither are they considered as infallible formulæ, by the enlightened Buddhist.

They constitute the ethical and moral code of the undeveloped man in all ages of the world, and among all peoples. They had become traditional long before Buddha came to interpret "the way of the gods." But Gautama, like Jesus, was an evolutionist, and not a revolutionist. He came "not to destroy, but to fulfill," and so Buddha paid no attention to the code of morals as it stood, but merely contented himself with emphasizing the importance of unselfishness—purity of heart and mind, because he realized that the mental world is the trap of the soul, even as "the elephant is held tethered by a galucchi creeper."

Buddha taught the way of emancipation of the soul held in bondage by means of the illusions of maya, even as the elephant is held in captivity by so weak a thing as a galucchi creeper, which could be broken by a single effort.

That many who keep the commandments are yet a long way from cosmic consciousness must be apparent to all. Therefore we are justified in assuming that the mere keeping of the commandments will not bring about mukti. Many a man follows the letter of the law, and escapes prison, but if he does this through fear of punishment, and not because of a desire to maintain peace that his neighbors may be benefited, then he is not keeping the spirit of the law at all, and his reward is a negative one.

According to the most reliable authorities, Buddha died in his eightieth year, having spent about fifty years in preaching, in healing the sick, in conversing with exalted beings in the heavenly worlds, and in leaving at will his physical body and visiting other worlds.

Buddha prophesied his coming dissolution, and expressed to his disciples, a hope that they would realize that he still lived, even when his physical body should have become ashes.

As his last hour approached, Buddha summoned his disciples, and after a moment's silent meditation, he addressed himself to Ananda, his relative; as well as his favorite disciple, thus:

"When I shall have disappeared from this state of existence, and be no longer with you, do not believe that the Buddha has left you, and ceased to dwell among you. Do not think therefore, nor believe, that the Buddha has disappeared, and is no more with you."

From these words, it is evident that the state of Nirvana which Buddha assured his followers that he had already attained, did not argue loss of identity, nor translation to another planet.

Nor is there anywhere in the sayings of Buddha, rightly interpreted, any suggestion of expecting or desiring personal worship. This, the great sage particularly avoided, as indeed have all illumined ones.

It is evident that Gautama the Buddha had experienced that divine influx of light and wisdom in which he sought for others the happiness he had gained for himself, and to this end he was eager to leave to his friends and disciples such rules of conduct of life as should aid them in attaining the divine peace that comes from illumination.

But that he founded a religious system of worship of himself, is wholly unbelievable in the light of a study of comparative religions and the wisdom which illumination confers.

To realize that one has attained to immortality, and claimed his birthright of godhood, is not synonymous with the claim to worship as the one eternal source of life.

It is a part of human weakness to insist upon idealizing the personality of a teacher, and this tendency becomes in time merged into actual worship, whereas the teacher, if he or she be truly illumined, seeks only to inculcate the philosophy which will bring his faithful followers into a realization of cosmic consciousness.

The points which characterize the person who has experienced a degree of illumination (entered into cosmic consciousness), were particularly evident in the life and character of Gautama, the Buddha. They may be summed up thus:

A marked seriousness in youth.

A great sympathy and compassion with the sorrows of others.

A deep tenderness for all forms of life.

A realization of the nothingness of caste and pomp and power.

The firm conviction that he was instructed by angels.

The wonderful magnetism and illumination of his person.

The firm conviction of immortality—released from the "wheel of life" as he expressed it.

The knowledge of when and where he was to pass out from the life of the body.

The love of solitude and meditation. The intellectual power maintained even into old age.

The unselfish desire to help others.

Great and never-failing sympathy with suffering, a divine patience, and insight into the hearts of all forms of life, earned for this great soul the name "Buddha—The Compassionate."

Chapter Nine - Jesus of Nazareth

Turning now to the next in order of the world's great masters, or illumined ones, we come to a consideration of Jesus of Nazareth, in whose name the great moral system of religion, called "Christianity," is promulgated.

It has been conclusively shown that the essential features of the present-day system of religion, known as Christianity, were instituted by Paul rather than by Jesus, and that the system itself, like Buddhism, is the work of the followers of the great teacher, rather than that of the Master.

Our present concern, however, is not with the system or method of the church, but with those historic facts which bear upon the question of the Illumination of Jesus, classifying Him, not as an incarnate son of God, in the accepted theological interpretation, but in the light of cosmic consciousness.

Jesus the Christ was born, according to the most reliable authorities, about six hundred years after Gautama, the Buddha.

Whether or not the Nazarene was familiar with the Buddhist doctrines or whether He spent the years of His life which are shrouded in mystery, in the inner temples of either Thibet, India, Persia, China, or other oriental country, will doubtless always be a disputed point among controversialists.

The fact does not matter, either way.

There is an encouraging similarity in the fundamentals of all religious precepts, arguing that when a teacher is really inspired, the truth makes friends with him or her.

Some writers on the subject of Illumination give exact dates when the flash of cosmic consciousness came to the various teachers of the world, but these dates are problematical, and they are also inconsequential.

That Jesus was among those historic characters who had attained cosmic consciousness, there can be no possible doubt, even though his exact words will be disputed.

Enough has come down to us through the ages to prove the fact that Jesus knew and taught the illusory character of external life (maya) and that he was himself absolutely certain of the "kingdom within," which he admonished his hearers to seek, rather than to live so much in the external. This he did because he well knew that constant dwelling in the external consciousness led not to liberation.

The light within, was the substance of his cry, and that light, when perceived, leads to illumination of everything, both the within and the without.

The transfiguration of Jesus was undoubtedly the effect of his being in a supra-conscious state, a state of exaltation, in which many mystics enter at more or less frequent intervals, according to their mode of life, and their objective environment.

"And he was transfigured before them; and his garments became exceedingly white," we are told in the gospels, and there are many persons in the world to-day possessing the power of the inner or clairvoyant vision (not identical with cosmic consciousness), who have witnessed similar phenomena.

In the "Sermon on the Mount," we find that Jesus spoke with such certainty and such authority, as one who had experienced the very essence of the cosmic conscious state, and was already freed from the illusions of the senses. His words, like those of all who have sought to give directions and instructions for the attainment of freedom from externality, are capable of interpretation in various ways, according to the degree of consciousness of the age in which the interpretations have been made.

For example, we find these words of Jesus given different meanings, and in fact, there have been many and diverse discussions and conclusions as to exactly what the Master did mean by them:

"Blessed are the poor in spirit, for theirs is the kingdom of heaven."

Let us examine the phrase, and see if it accords with our ideas of cosmic consciousness. To be "poor in spirit," is not consistent with our understanding of the requirements for the expansion of the soul.

Those who take this phrase literally, and who are opposed to religious concepts, as a factor in human betterment, are fond of using this phrase as an evidence of the fanaticism of Jesus, and his concurrence in the worldly habit of exploiting the poor, and "riding the backs of the wage slaves," as our Socialist brothers put it.

Now let us, for a moment, consider the phrase as a person who possessed cosmic consciousness would have said it.

One possessing the cosmic sense, viewing the external more as a trap of the senses, than as realities, would readily perceive that to amass wealth (external possessions), the mind must be in harmony with the methods and the ideals of the world, rather than that it should be concentrated upon the "things of the spirit."

This idea is expressed in the phrase, "no man can serve two masters," and while we are not prepared to say that the possession of worldly goods is absolutely impossible to the attainment of cosmic consciousness—observation, reflection, and intuition will unite in the conclusion that they are more or less improbable.

If then, we will interpret these sayings of Jesus in the light of a broader outlook than was possible to the understanding of his chroniclers, we will find that what he doubtless said was:

"Blessed in spirit are the poor, for theirs shall be the kingdom of heaven."

And in his vision, which extended beyond the times in which he lived, and foresaw that the attainment of cosmic consciousness must involve a degree of physical hardship, he said:

"Blessed are they that have been persecuted for righteousness' sake, for theirs is the kingdom of heaven."

A survey of the world's progress will readily prove the fact that those who have bent their talents and their energies toward the uplift of the race, have done so under great stress, and in the face of persistent opposition.

This opposition is an accompaniment to altruistic effort, for the very obvious reason that the race-thought of the world is still materialistic.

The thoughts that predominate are commercial. This is due to the fact that those who are wealthy have large financial interests to maintain; business problems to solve; that take about all their time. The poor find the maintenance of physical existence a task that absorbs the greater part of their mortal mind, and therefore, those who are devoting their time and talents to the work of regeneration (the coming of the cosmic sense), are necessarily in the minority, and the majority rules in thought, as in act.

The present metaphysical movement lays great stress upon worldly success and "attraction" of wealth, as an evidence of possession of power and truth, but the law of equation proves that we obtain that which we most desire. A religious system which amasses great wealth in a short time does so, only because its dominant teaching inspires the desire for worldly advancement, as the prime requisite.

The same is true of an individual, as of a system.

Not that the attainment of cosmic consciousness is absolutely impossible to a rich man, because a man may inherit riches and position and power, as in the case of Prince Siddhartha, the Lord Buddha; or he may have set in motion certain currents of desire for wealth, and later in life may change that desire, when naturally, the "business" he has created will follow the law which instigated it, and increasing wealth will result.

But, let it be known, that Buddha renounced all his possessions, and there are many instances to-day of renunciation of worldly life and wealth, in order to attain to that supreme consciousness in which the illumined one possesses all that he desires, even though he have but one coat to his back.

Let it not be thought that we mean to infer that God is partial to poverty, and that the rich man will be excluded from the attainment of the kingdom, merely because of his riches; but if riches be any man's aim, then assuredly he cannot "serve two masters" and it will not be possible for him to become illumined while in pursuit of worldly goods.

Jesus said:

"It is easier for a camel to go through the needle's eye, than for a rich man to enter the kingdom of heaven."

It is now thoroughly established that the "Needle's Eye" was the name given to a certain narrow and difficult pass through which camels bearing heavy burdens, could not find room to pass, and Jesus sought to convey to his hearers the truth that persons bearing in their mental desires the load of many possessions, would hardly find room for the one supreme desire which would bring them into the kingdom (the possession of cosmic consciousness).

But the most significant of the utterances of the illumined Nazarene is the one in which he said:

"Except ye become as little children, ye can in no wise enter the kingdom of heaven."

The possession of cosmic consciousness brings with it, invariably, the simplicity, the faith and innocence of a little child. The child is pleased with natural pleasures, and does not know the worldly standard of valuation. And above all, the soul, while still attached to the physical body, is like a little child.

The attainment of cosmic consciousness is possible only to one who has first "got acquainted with his soul"; when we are really soul-conscious we possess the innocence (not ignorance), of a little child, and we also possess a child's wisdom. We are, in other words, "as wise as the serpent and as harmless as the dove." Wisdom brings with it harmlessness. The truly wise person would not wilfully harm any living thing; wisdom knows no revenge; no "eye for an eye" philosophy; makes no demands.

And what may be considered the second most significant remark of the Master is this:

"The kingdom of God cometh not with observation; neither shall they say Lo, here; or Lo, there, for Lo, the kingdom of heaven is within you."

Jesus, although forced by the conventions of the time in which he taught to conform to the laws laid down by the scribes and Pharisees, influenced by the strict views of the Israelites, who honored the law laid down by Moses and the prophets, still possessed cosmic consciousness to such an extent that he knew the folly of judging others by outward appearance, and also of promising them cosmic consciousness in return for obedience to prescribed rules or commandments.

When it would seem to his critics that he did not sufficiently emphasize the traditional laws, that he was seemingly making it too simple and too easy for people to live, they sought to trap him into a statement that would oppose the accepted commandments.

But this Jesus steadfastly refused to do. "I came not to destroy the law, but to fulfill it," he said.

Like all those who have experienced cosmic consciousness, his policy was one of construction, and not of destruction. Evolution accomplishes peacefully what revolution seeks to do by force.

Jesus laid little stress upon the commandments as they stood. He neither sought to emphasize them, nor to criticise them. All that he said was:

"A new commandment give I unto you: that ye love one another."

All truly illumined minds have made love the basis of their teaching, well knowing that where true love reigns there can be no destruction.

Love conquers fear—the arch-enemy of mankind.

Love makes it impossible to harm the thing loved, and universal love would make it impossible, for one experiencing it, to consciously bring the slightest pain to any living thing.

Therefore Jesus taught repeatedly the doctrine of love, and he made no new commandments other than this.

It has been said that inasmuch as Jesus laid greater emphasis upon this one great need than had any previous inspired teacher, he deserves greater honor.

Theologians whose purpose it is to promulgate the doctrine of Christianity as superior to others, use this argument in support of their contention that Jesus was the only true son of God.

But this view will be recognized as prejudiced, and lacking in the very essentials taught and practiced by the Christ.

In the light of Illumination, it will readily be perceived that all persons expressing any considerable degree of cosmic consciousness, have taught the same fundamental and simple truths, as witness the following:

Do as you would be done by.—Persian.

Do not that to a neighbor which you would take ill from him.—Grecian.

What you would not wish done to yourself, do not unto others.—Chinese.

One should seek for others the happiness one desires for oneself.—Buddhist.

He sought for others the good he desired for himself. Let him pass on.—Egyptian.

All things whatsoever ye would that men should do to you, do you even so to them.—Christian.

Let none of you treat his brother in a way he himself would dislike to be treated.—Mohammedan.

The true rule in life is to guard and do by the things of others as they do by their own.—Hindu.

The law imprinted on the hearts of all men is to love the members of society as themselves.—Roman.

Whatsoever you do not wish your neighbor to do to you, do not unto him. This is the whole law. The rest is a mere exposition of it.—Jewish.

While it is probable that Jesus gave no directions or methods of attainment, yet the records of his sayings give the clue to the character of his instruction to those of his students who were capable of understanding, particularly as shown in a recently discovered papyrus, authentically identified as belonging to the early Christians. This-papyrus was discovered by Egyptian explorers in 1904. Although the papyrus was more or less mutilated, the meaning is sufficiently clear to justify the translators in inserting certain words. However, we will here quote only such of the "sayings" as were decipherable, without having anything supplied by translators.

Evidently having been asked when his kingdom should be realized on earth he answered:

"When ye return to the state of innocence which existed before the fall" (i.e., when manifestation will be perceived in its illusory character, and the soul freed from the enchantment of the mortal consciousness).

"I am come to end the sacrifices and if ye cease not from sacrificing, the wrath shall not cease from you."

This evidently corresponds to his saying, "They who use the sword, shall perish by the sword."

The conclusion is obvious that hate and destruction beget their kind, and that love is the only power that can prevent the continuation of destruction. This may with equal logic, be applied to the sacrifice of animal and bird life for food, as well as the sacrifices of blood which formed a part of ancient ritual.

His disciples said unto him:

"When will thou be manifest to us, and when shall we see thee?"

He saith:

"When ye shall be stripped and not be ashamed."

The time is near at hand, when the body will not be regarded as something vile and unworthy; something of which to be ashamed and to keep covered, as if God's handiwork were vile.

In fact, the function of sex, from the extreme of ancient sex worship to the present extreme of sex degradation, shall soon be established in its rightful place. It is not the purpose of this book to deal with this important subject, so we will say no more here.

Nevertheless, this saying attributed to Jesus, the Christ, resurrected as it has been in this century, is timely. It is almost universally conceded that the time of the "Second Coming of Christ" is already at hand. Just what this second coming means, is interpreted differently by theologians, philosophers, scientists, poets and prophets, but there is a unanimous belief that the time is here and now.

Those who have the comprehension to read the signs of the times, are cheerfully expectant of radical changes in our attitude toward the function of sex and the divinity of love.

"When the two shall be one, and the outside as the inside, and the male as the female, neither male nor female—these things if ye do, the kingdom of My Father shall come."

Again, the meaning of these words depends upon the degree of illumination of the person reading them. They mean the present inevitable equality of the sexes, when each individual will count not as a mere man or a mere woman, but as an important factor in the world's redemption. Or, it will appeal to a few as the promised time when every soul which has completed the circle, ended its karma, and claimed its god-hood, unites with the soul of its mate, the two blending into one perfect whole—the Father-Mother God of the New Dispensation.

Again we find in these newly discovered papyri a phrase bearing upon this subject:

To the question of Salome:

"How long shall death reign?" The Lord answered:

"As long as ye women give birth. For I am come to make an end to the works of the woman."

Then Salome said to him:

"Then have I done well that I have not given birth?"

To this the Lord replied:

"Eat of every herb, but of the bitter one eat not."

When Salome asked when it shall be known what she asked, the Lord said:

"When you tread under foot the covering of shame, and when two is made one, and the male with the female, neither male nor female."

"How be it, he who longs to be rich is like a man who drinketh sea water: the more he drinketh the more thirsty he becomes, and never leaves off drinking till he perish."

"Blessed is he who also fasts that he may feed the poor, for it is more blessed to give than to receive."

"Let thy alms sweat in thy hand until thou knowest to whom thou givest."

It is not probable that any one who reads these words will make the mistake of assuming that Jesus advised us to inquire into the character or the antecedents of the one on whom we are to bestow a gift. Neither are we expected to ascertain whether he belongs to our "lodge" or not.

If you give alms as though to an inferior; if you assume a self-righteous mind; if you give for hope of reward; then withhold your gift. In fact, unless you can realize that you are giving as though to yourself, keep your gift. It will do neither you nor the one receiving it, any good whatsoever.

"Good things must come. He is blessed through whom they come."

This presages the coming of the kingdom of love on earth, as a foregone conclusion. Yet, those who lend themselves consciously, as servants of the cause—helpers in the establishment of the new order—are blessed.

"Love covereth a multitude of sins, so be not joyful save when you look upon your brother's countenance in love."

"Let not the sun go down upon your wrath, for the greatest of crimes is this: if a man shall sadden his brother's spirit."

"For our possessions are in heaven; therefore, sons of men, purchase unto yourselves by these transitory things which are not yours, what is yours, and shall not pass away."

For the Lord has said in a mystery: "Unless ye make the right as the left; the left as the right; the top as the bottom; and the front as the backward, ye shall not know the kingdom of God."

"Keep the flesh holy and the seal undented, that ye may receive eternal life."

"If a man shall sadden his brother's spirit." This indeed is the greatest of all crimes, because out of man's inhumanity to man springs all the sin and sorrow of the world.

"Unless ye make the right as the left; the top as the bottom; the front as the backward." The meaning should be clear enough and the words are worthy of the illumined mind of Jesus of Nazareth.

The great sin is separation; segregation; "My and mine" as opposed to "Thee and thine." To the truly illumined one there can be no "mine," as distinct from another's.

The sinner is no less my brother than is the saint. The beggar is as dear to me as is the rich man. Every man is a king. There are no "chosen of God" to the one who has entered cosmic consciousness.

"For our possessions are in heaven. Use, therefore, the things of earth, while ye are living in the flesh (sons of men), in such a way and to such purpose that they will not enchain you in the maze of manifestation, and thereby require that you postpone your claim to immortality."

This statement is distinct enough, as is also the one: "He who longs to be rich is like a man drinking sea water. The more he drinketh, the more thirsty he becomes and never leaves off drinking until he perisheth."

The hypnotism of the external world is too well illustrated to need further comment. The man who enters upon the pursuit of worldly possessions; temporal power; personal ambition; thinking that when he shall have attained all these, then will he turn to the solution of the mystery of mysteries, finds himself caught in the trap of his desires, and he can not escape. He is under the spell of enchantment, wherein the unreal appears as real, and the real becomes the illusory.

To sum up, the fragmentary accounts we have of the life and character of the man Jesus are conclusive proof that he had entered into full realization of cosmic consciousness.

Like Lord Gautama, he appeared to his disciples after he had left the physical body, "glorified," as one who had taken on immortality.

Nor was there ever, it would appear, any doubt in the mind of Jesus, of his right to godhood, while retaining, also, his self-consciousness.

The intellectual superiority.

The wonderful spiritual magnetism and attraction of his presence.

The absolute, unwavering conviction of his mission, and of his immortality.

The transfiguration, after his "temptation" and his prophetic vision.

His great love and compassion for even his enemies.

These are what made him indeed a Christ.

The term "Christ" and the term "Buddha" are synonymous. They both mean one who has entered into his godhood. One who has attained to cosmic consciousness, leaving forever the limitations of the lower self.

Chapter Ten - Paul of Tarsus

The system of worship known as Christianity owes its systematic foundation to Paul of Tarsus. Paul's sudden conversion from zealous persecution of the followers of Jesus of Nazareth to an equally zealous propaganda of the gospel of Light, offers a perfect example of the peculiar oncoming of cosmic consciousness.

Paul evidently occupied a position of authority among the Jews and it is equally probable that he was near the same age as Jesus, as he is referred to as a "young man named Saul" in Bible accounts of the persecution of the early Christians. His illumination occurred shortly after the crucifixion, probably within two or three years.

In Acts, chapter 8-9, we read:

"And Saul was consenting unto his death (Stephen). And at that time there was a great persecution against the church which was at Jerusalem and they were all scattered abroad throughout the regions of Judea, and Samaria, except the apostles.

"And devout men carried Stephen to his burial, and made great lamentation over him.

"As for Saul, he made havoc of the church, entering into every house, and hailing men and women, committed them to prison.

"And Saul, yet breathing out threatenings, and slaughter against the disciples of the Lord, went unto the high priest and desired of him letters to Damascus to the synagogues, that if he found any of this way, whether they were men or women, he might bring them bound, unto Jerusalem.

"And as he journeyed he came near unto Damascus, and suddenly there shone round about him a light from heaven.

"And he fell to the earth and heard a voice saying unto him: 'Saul, Saul, why persecutest thou me?'

"And he said: 'Who art thou, Lord?' And the Lord said: 'I am Jesus, whom thou persecutest; it is hard for thee to kick against the pricks.'

"And he trembling and astonished, said: 'Lord, what wilt thou have me do?'

"And the Lord said unto him: 'Arise and go into the city, and it shall be told thee what thou must do.'

"And the men which journeyed with him stood speechless, hearing a voice but seeing no man.

"And Saul arose from the earth, and when his eyes were opened he saw no man; but they led him by the hand and brought him into Damascus.

"And he was three days without sight and neither did eat nor drink.

"And there was a certain disciple at Damascus, named Ananias, and to him said the Lord in a vision: 'Ananias;' and he said: 'Lord, behold, I am here.' And the Lord said unto him: 'Arise and go into the street called Straight, and enquire in the house of Judas for one called Saul of Tarsus; for behold, he prayeth. And hath seen in a vision a man named Ananias coming in and putting his hand on him that he might receive his sight.' Then Ananias answered: 'Lord, I have heard by many of this man, how much evil he hath done by thy saints at Jerusalem. And here he hath authority from the high priests to bind all that call on thy name.' But the Lord said unto him: 'Go thy way; for he is a chosen vessel unto me, to bear my name before the Gentiles, and kings, and children of Israel. For I will show him how great things he must suffer for my name's sake.'

"And Ananias went his way, and entered into the house; and putting his hands on him, said: 'Brother Saul, the Lord, even Jesus, that appeared unto thee in the way as thou camest, hath sent me, that thou mightest receive thy sight, and be filled with the Holy Ghost.' And immediately there fell from his eyes, as it had been scales; and he received sight forthwith, and arose and was baptized."

Like all those who have entered cosmic consciousness, Paul sought the blessing of solitude, that he might readjust himself to his changed viewpoint, since he now saw things in the light of the larger consciousness.

He says:

"Immediately I conferred, not with flesh and blood; neither went I up to Jerusalem to them which were apostles before me; but I went away into Arabia; and again I returned unto Damascus."

The irresistible longing to get away from the sights and sounds of the external world, is one of the most characteristic phases of Illumination. It is only in order that they may take up the work of bringing to others this great blessing that those who have entered into the larger consciousness, eventually bring themselves to enter the life of the world.

Thus, we find that Paul's great desire to bring the light to others, took him again to Damascus; and from the records we have of his utterances and his mode of living, we may gather some idea of the great change which Illumination made in him.

Certain statements, which characterize all who possess cosmic consciousness, in any degree of fullness, emanate from the converted Paul. He says:

"I must needs glory though it is not expedient, but I will come to visions and revelations of the Lord—for if I should desire to glory I shall not be foolish; for I shall speak the truth; but I forbear, lest any man should account of me above that which he seeth me to be, or heareth from me. And by reason of the exceeding greatness of the revelations—wherefore that I should not be exalted overmuch, there was given to me a thorn in the flesh, a messenger of Satan to buffet me."

One of the characteristics of the Illumined is a deep humility. This is not in any sense an abasement of the self; not in any sense a feeling that it is necessary to "bow down and worship;" nor yet a tinge of that nameless fear, which the carnal-minded self feels in the presence of exalted beings.

It is a humility born of the desire to make every one know and feel a sense of kinship with him; he hesitates to reveal all that has been revealed to him, lest those who hear his words may think he is either "speaking foolishly," through egotism, or else that they may look upon him as a being superior, more exalted, than themselves. And a divine compassion and love for his fellow being characterizes the Illumined. Again, Paul wishes to make clear the fact that he is still living in the physical body; living the life of a body, and until liberated from the conditions that influence the external world, he is himself subject to the lesser consciousness, and he does not want them to expect more of the personal self, than that personal self is capable of, under the conditions in which he lives.

He desires no personal exaltation, or praise, therefore he hesitates to speak fully of his own revelations, but prefers to teach by reference to the experiences of others.

Nevertheless, he tries to make clear the fact that he is not merely preaching a "belief," which he has embraced because of doubt or fear, or because it is a creed. Indeed, he is free from the "law" and is, therefore, not merely following a system, neither the old one which he has abandoned, nor a new one which he has accepted. He speaks from the "Lord," which is no other than the highest authority that man may know—namely, the authority that comes from the realization of his own imperishable godhood—the effect of cosmic consciousness.

He says:

"For I make known to you brethren, as touching the gospel as preached by me, that it is not after man. For neither did I receive it from man, nor was I taught it, but it came to me through revelation of Christ.

"Christ redeemed us from the curse of the law. But before faith came, we were kept inward under the law, shut up unto the faith which should afterwards be revealed. For ye are all sons of God through faith in Christ. For with freedom did Christ set us free."

This we take to refer to his former adherence to, and belief in, the system of worship taught by the Jews, as a necessary and probably the only "way of salvation" acceptable to God. He wishes his hearers to understand that he is not bound by adherence to any creed; neither the old one, nor yet the new one, but that what he preached came from the light of cosmic consciousness, in which there is no law, nor sense of law. Cosmic consciousness gives to the illumined one a sense of freedom (Christ means cosmic consciousness, and not a personality).

Cosmic consciousness confers, above all else, perhaps, a sense of freedom from every form of bondage.

The duty and the obligations that bind the average person, are impossible to the cosmically conscious one. Not that he displays indifference toward the welfare and the rights of others. Far from that, he feels an added sense of responsibility for the irresponsible; an overwhelming compassion for the unfortunate, and a relationship greater than ever to mankind.

But this sense of freedom causes him to do all in love, which he hitherto did because it was so "laid down in the law."

Again St. Paul makes this plain:

"The fruit of the spirit is love, joy, peace, long suffering, kindness, goodness, faithfulness, meekness, temperance; against such as these there is no law—neither is circumcision anything, nor uncircumcision, but a new creature."

When we are armored with the "fruit of the spirit," we have no need for rules of conduct; for methods of salvation; or for any of the bonds that are necessary to the merely sense-conscious man.

Plainly, Paul recognized the fact that systems of religion, of philosophy, of rules and ethics of intercourse, are necessary only so long as man remains on the sense-conscious plane. When Illumination comes, there comes with it absolute freedom. God does not want to be worshipped on bended knee; by rites and ceremonies; by obedience to commandments, but the undisciplined soul acquires power and poise through these exercises, and in time grows to the full stature of god-consciousness.

Nor is intellectual greatness to be confounded with the godlike character of the one who has attained to Illumination.

Elsewhere in these pages we have made the distinction between knowledge and wisdom. Knowledge alone can never bring a soul into the path of Illumination. Wisdom will point the way, but love is the unerring guide to the very goal.

St. Paul's expression of this fact is concise, and to the point. This observation alone, stamps him as one possessing a very high degree of realization of what cosmic consciousness is.

"If any man thinketh that he is wise among you in this world, let him become a fool that he may become wise. For the wisdom of this world is foolishness to God."

The worldly wise man or woman asks "how much do I get?" The truly wise person cares nothing at all for possessions. He only asks "how much can I give?"

And although we find in the marts of commercialism a contempt for the gullible, and the credulous; the trusting and the confiding, let it be known that the "smart" bargainer will indeed smart for his smartness, for in the light of cosmic consciousness, this alleged "wisdom" of men, appears as utter foolishness; wasted effort; a perversion of opportunity.

Because "all these things shall pass away."

Love alone is imperishable.

Love alone is the savior of the human race, and whenever we fail to act from motives of love, we are disloyal to the light within us.

Again says St. Paul:

"If I speak with the tongues of men and of angels, and have not love, I am as sounding brass and a tinkling cymbal.

"And if I have the gift of prophecy, and know all mysteries and all knowledge; and if I have all faith, so as to remove mountains, but have not love, I am nothing.

"And if I bestow all my goods to feed the poor, and if I give my body to be burned, but have not love, it profiteth me nothing.

"LOVE NEVER FAILETH.

"But whether there be prophecies they shall be done away; whether there be tongues they shall cease; whether there be knowledge it shall be done away. For we know in part and we prophecy in part, but when that which is perfect is come, that which is in part shall be done away."

It must be remembered that in the days of St. Paul the high priests and the prophets were accounted the wisest and most exalted persons in the community.

The ability to prophecy presupposed a special favor of the God of the Jews. St. Paul's exposition of the changed viewpoint that comes to one who has entered into cosmic consciousness, was therefore aptly illustrated by his open avowal that there was a far greater power—a more exalted state of consciousness, than that of the gift of prophecy and of "knowing all mysteries;" that state of one in which love was the ruler, and in order that they might the more fully comprehend the simplicity, and yet the perfection, of this state of consciousness, he made clear the fact that no one truly who became "a new creature", as he characterized this change, ever exalted himself, or made high claims; or became exclusive, or "superior," or "holy," in the sense the latter word had been used.

How, then, would they know when they had attained to this state of consciousness, of which he spoke, and which they but dimly understood?

How might they know when they had found this great love that was to make them "a new creature"?

First of all, they might know because:

LOVE NEVER FAILETH.

Love suffereth long and is kind; love envieth not; love vaunteth not itself; is not puffed up, does not behave unseemly; seeketh not its own; is not provoked; taketh not account of evil; rejoiceth not in unrighteousness, but rejoiceth with the truth; beareth all things; believeth all things; hopeth all things; endureth all things.

In fact, LOVE NEVER FAILETH. Love is always a safe guide. No matter what may be said to the contrary; no matter how much suffering it entails; no matter how seemingly fruitless the sacrifice; or how ungrateful the results, love never faileth.

How can it fail when we "seek not our own," but only love for love's own sake, without regard to compensation or gratitude?

St. Paul, with all who have expressed in any considerable degree this cosmic realization, seems to have expected a time, when cosmic consciousness should become so general, as to bring the kingdom of love upon earth. This corresponds to the Millenium, which has always been prophesied, and which the present era fulfills, in all the "signs of the times" that were to usher in The Dawn.

Moreover, the idea that there shall come a time when death shall be overcome, is a persistent part of every prophecy, and of every religious cult. In these days we find that science is speculating upon the probability of discovering a specific for senile death, as well as for the final elimination of death from disease and accidents.

Whether or not this is to be the manner of "overcoming the last enemy," the fact remains that the almost universally held idea of physical immortality has a basis in fact, which this postulate of science symbolizes.

"For this corruptible must put on incorruption, and this mortality must put on immortality, but when this corruptible shall have put on incorruption, and this mortal shall have put on immortality, then shall come to pass the saying that is written: 'Death is swallowed up in victory.'"

So said St. Paul, and his words show clearly that before his time there had been a prophecy and belief in the final triumph of love over death, not as an article of faith, but as a common knowledge.

St. Paul speaks of the time when "we shall not all sleep, but we shall all be changed, in a moment, in the twinkling of an eye, at the last trump.

"And then come to the end, when he shall deliver up the kingdom to God, even the Father; when he shall have abolished all rule, all authority, and all power."

Unquestionably, if all men on earth in the flesh and in the astral, were to come into the light of the cosmic consciousness, there would be no need for laws, for authority or power. The kingdom, which signifies the earth as a planet, would indeed be delivered to God, which means Love, and "Love never faileth."

And while we admit that these words of St. Paul may be applied to individual attainment of cosmic consciousness, and not refer to an era of earth life, in which the fruits of this larger consciousness are to be gathered in the physical, yet we maintain that the argument for such an hypothesis is strong indeed. He says:

"For the earnest expectation of creation waiteth for the revealing of the sons of God."

For the term "sons of God" interpret "those who have attained cosmic consciousness," and we may readily parallel this with the many allusions to the earth's redemption, with which history is strewn.

To "redeem" the earth is quite comparable with the idea of redeeming any part of the earth's surface—either as a nation, or as a tract of land—which is not yielding the best that it is capable of.

In the cosmogony of the heavens, the planet earth may well be likened to a territory that has possibilities, but which needs cultivation; encouragement; work; to bring out its possibilities and make it a place of comfort and enlightenment.

So we have been informed—and an understanding of deeper occultism will bear out the information—that this earth is being made a "fit habitation for the gods" (i.e., cosmically conscious beings, to whom love is the only authority necessary).

Paul clearly alludes to the redemption of the body, as well as the continuance of the life of the soul, when he says:

"For the creation was subject to vanity, not of its own will, but by reason of him who subjected it, in hope that the creation itself also shall be delivered from the bondage of corruption into the liberty of the glory of the children of God. For we know that the whole creation groaneth and travaileth in pain together until now. And not only so, but ourselves also, WHICH HAVE THE FIRST FRUITS OF THE SPIRIT, even we ourselves, waiting for our adoption, to wit, the redemption of the body."

St. Paul declared that even those who had glimpsed that wonderful Illumination (which have the first fruits of the spirit), are not free from the travail of the sense-conscious world, until such time as the cycle has been completed, and those who "are already in Christ, and then they that are Christ's at his coming," shall have made possible the perfected creation, and brought about the reign of love on earth.

So that, when a sufficient number of souls shall have attained to this Illumination (cosmic consciousness), the "last enemy shall be overcome."

That this present era gives promise of this hope, is evident.

The attainment of cosmic consciousness brings with it immunity from reincarnation, as a necessity—as a law, but it does not provide against the coming of avatars—"sons of God," who are to "deliver Creation from the bondage of corruption."

This also is clearly stated by Paul:

"There is no condemnation to them that are in Christ. For the law of the spirit of life in Christ made me free from the law of sin and death."

There never is any doubt in the minds of those who have attained cosmic consciousness, that they are spiritual beings and immortal—free from the law of karma; neither is there any thought of evil or of condemnation.

They know that men are gods in embryo and that until they have been born into the cosmic consciousness—the realization of their reality as spirit, they must travail; but this sense-conscious state is not to be condemned any more than the child is to be condemned because it has not yet grown to adultship.

The advice of St. Paul himself was simple enough and straight-forward enough. It was devoid of all subtleties; free from complexity; free from fear, or haste, or doubt, or strife, while confidently awaiting the universal attainment of Illumination.

To the question as to what path to follow; what should be done to gain this great boon, if the law of the ancient Hebrews was not to be followed in its literal significance, Paul said:

"Whatsoever things are honest; whatsoever things are true; whatsoever things are just; whatsoever things are pure; whatsoever things are lovely; whatsoever things are of good report; if there be any virtue, and if there be any praise, THINK ON THESE THINGS."

Which is to say, do not seek the letter of the way of Illumination. Do not look for forms and ceremonies and rules and systems, but look for that which is clean and pure and good wherever it may be found.

In St. Paul we have fulfilled all the points that characterize those who have been blessed with the great Illumination.

His broad outlook upon humanity, which refused to see evil or to condemn where formerly he had been noted for his zeal in bringing to condemnation all whom he believed to be heretics; his conviction of immortality; his humility, as far as personal aggrandizement was concerned; the great light in which was revealed to him the truth; the annihilation of the idea of sin and death; the realization that systems and laws and methods of worship and giving of alms and all the by-paths which formerly he had deemed necessary, were as naught compared to the great illuminating, all-embracing power of Love—the Savior whose kingdom should sometime be established upon earth—the time being when cosmic consciousness should be general.

Chapter Eleven – Mohammed

Despite the fact that the followers of Mohammed, the prophet, are among the most fanatical and prejudiced of all religious sects, Mohammed himself was unquestionably among the Illumined Ones of earth, and had attained and retained a high degree of cosmic consciousness.

The wars; the persecutions; the horrors that have been committed in the name of Islam, are perhaps a little more atrocious than any in history although the unspeakable cruelties of the Inquisition would seem to have no parallel.

The religion of Persia, wrongly alluded to as "fire-worship," marks Zoroaster as among the Illuminati, but as the present volume is concerned, in the religious aspect of it, only with those cases of Illumination which we are classifying among the present great religious systems, we cite the case of Mohammed, the Arab, as one clearly establishing the characteristic points of Illumination.

When Mohammed was born, in the early part of the fifth century, the condition of his countrymen was primitive in the extreme.

The most powerful force among them was tribal or clan loyalty, and a corresponding hatred of, and readiness to make war with, opposing clans.

Although at the time of Mohammed's birth, Christianity had made great headway in different parts of the old world, it had made very little impress upon the Arabs. They worshipped their tribal gods, and there are traces of a belief in a supreme God (Allah ta-ala), but they were not as a race inclined to a deeply religious sentiment.

One and all, whether given to superstitions or denying a belief in Allah, they dreaded the dark after-life and although the different tribes made their yearly pilgrimages to Mecca, and faithfully kissed the stone that had fallen from heaven in the days of Adam, the inspiration of their ancient prophets had long since died, and a new prophet was expected and looked for.

The yearly pilgrimage to Mecca, which was at once the center of trade and the goal of the religious enthusiast, was observed by all the tribes of Arabia, but it is a question whether the pilgrimage was not more often made in a holiday spirit than in that of the devotee to the Kaabeh, the most sacred temple in all Arabia.

Indeed, it is agreed by all commentators, that the ancient Arab, "In the Time of Ignorance," before the coming of Mohammed, knew little and cared less about those spiritual qualities that look beyond the physical; not questioning, as did Mohammed, what lies beyond this vale of strife, whose only exit is the dark and inscrutable face of death.

Besides the tribal gods, individual households had their special Penates, to whom was due the first and the last salam of the returning or out-going host. But in spite of all this superstitious apparatus, the Arabs were never a religious people. In the old days, as now, they were reckless, skeptical, materialistic. They had their gods and their divining arrows, but they were ready to demolish both if the responses proved contrary to their wishes. A great majority believed in no future life, nor in a reckoning day of good and evil.

Such, then, was the condition of thought among the various tribes when Mohammed was born.

It was not, however, until he was past forty years of age, that the revelations came to him, and although it was some time later that these were set down, together with his admonitions and counsel to his followers, it is believed that they are for the most part well authenticated, as the Koran was compiled during Mohammed's lifetime, and thus, in the original, doubtless represents an authentic account of Mohammed's experiences.

It is related that Mohammed's father died before his son's birth and his mother six years later. Thus Mohammed was left to the care of his grandfather, the virtual chief of Mecca. The venerable chief lived but two years and Mohammed, who was a great favorite with his grandfather, became the special charge of his uncle, Aboo-Talib, whose devotion never wavered, even during the trying later years, when Mohammed's persecutions caused the uncle untold hardships and trials.

At an early age Mohammed took up the life of a sheep herder, caring for the herds of his kinsmen. This step became necessary because the once princely fortune of his noble ancestors had dwindled to almost the extreme of poverty, but although the occupation of sheep herder was despised by the tribes, it is said that Mohammed himself in later life often alluded to his early calling as the time when "God called him."

At the age of twenty-five he took up the more desirable post of camel driver, and was taken into the employ of a wealthy kinswoman, Khadeejeh, whom he afterwards married, although she was fifteen years his senior—a disparity in age which means far more in the East, where physical charm and beauty are the only requisites for a wife, than it does in the West where men look more to the mental endowments of a wife than to the fleeting charm of youth.

It is also to Mohammed's credit that his devotion to his first wife never wavered to the day of her death and, indeed, as long as he himself lived he spoke with reverence and deep affection of Khadeejeh.

We learn that the next fifteen years were lived in the usual manner of a man of his station. Khadeejeh brought him wealth and this gave him the necessary time and ease in which to meditate, and the never-varying devotion and trust of his faithful wife brought him repose and the power to aid his impoverished uncle, and to be regarded among the tribes as a man of influence.

His simple, unostentatious, and even ascetic life during these years was noted. He was known as a man of extremely refined tastes and sensitive though not querulous nature. A commentator says of him:

"His constitution was extremely delicate. He was nervously afraid of bodily pain; he would sob and roar under it. Eminently unpractical in the common things of life, he was gifted with mighty powers of imagination, elevation of mind, delicacy and refinement of feeling.

"He is more modest than a virgin behind her curtain," it has been said of him.

"He was most indulgent to his inferiors and would not allow his awkward little page to be scolded, whatever he did. He was most affectionate toward his family. He was very fond of children, and would stop them in the streets and pat their little cheeks. He never struck anyone in his life. The worst expression he ever made use of in conversation was: 'What has come to him—may his forehead be darkened with mud.'

"When asked to curse some one he replied: 'I have not been sent to curse, but to be a mercy to mankind.' He visited the sick, followed any bier he met, accepted the invitation of a slave to dinner, mended his own clothes, milked his goats and waited upon himself.

"He never withdrew his hand out of another's palm, and turned not before the other had turned.

"He was the most faithful protector of those he protected, the sweetest and most agreeable in conversation; those who saw him were suddenly filled with reverence; those who came to him, loved him. They who described him would say: 'I have never seen his like, either before or after.'

"He was, however, very nervous and restless withal, often low-spirited, downcast as to heart and eyes. Yet he would at times suddenly break through these broodings, become gay, talkative, jocular, chiefly among his own."

This picture corresponds with the temperament which is alluded to as the "artistic," or "psychic" temperament, and allowing that in these days there is much posing and pretense, we still must admit that the quality known as "temperament" is a psychological study suggesting a stage of development hitherto unclassified. It is said also, that in his youth Mohammed was subject to attacks of catalepsy, evidencing an organism peculiarly "psychic."

It is evident that Mohammed regarded himself as one having a mission upon earth, even before he had received the revelations which announced him as a prophet chosen of Allah, for he long brooded over the things of the spirit, and although he had not, up to his fortieth year, openly protested against the fetish worship of the Kureysh, yet he was regarded as one who had a different idea of worship from that of the men with whom he came in contact.

Gradually, he became more and more inclined to solitude, and made frequent excursions into the hills, and in his solitary wanderings, he suffered agonies of doubt and self distrust, fearing lest he be self-deceived, and again, lest he be indeed called to become a prophet of God and fail in his mission.

Here in a cave, the revelation came. Mohammed had spent nights and days in fasting and prayer beseeching God for some sign, some word that would settle his doubts and agonies of distrust and longing for an answer to life's riddle.

It is related that suddenly during the watches of the night, Mohammed awoke to find his solitary cave filled with a great and wondrous light out of which issued a voice saying: "Cry, cry aloud." "What shall I cry?" he answers, and the voice answered:

"Cry in the name of thy Lord who hath created; He hath created man from a clot of blood. Cry—and thy Lord is the most bountiful, who hath taught by the pen; He hath taught man that which he knew not."

It is reported that almost immediately, Mohammed felt his intelligence illuminated with the light of spiritual understanding, and all that had previously vexed his spirit with doubt and non-comprehension, was clear as crystal to his understanding. Nevertheless, this feeling of assurance did not remain with him at that time, definitely, for we are told that "Mohammed arose trembling and went to Khadeejeh and told her what he had seen and heard; and she did her woman's part and believed in him and soothed his terror and bade him hope for the future. Yet he could not believe in himself. Was he not perhaps, mad? or possessed by a devil? Were these voices of a truth from God? And so he went again on the solitary wanderings, hearing strange sounds, and thinking them at one time the testimony of heaven and at another the temptings of Satan, or the ravings of madness. Doubting, wondering, hoping, he had fain put an end to a life which had become intolerable in its changings from the hope of heaven to the hell of despair, when he again heard the voice: 'Thou art the messenger of God and I am Gabriel.' Conviction at length seized hold upon him; he was indeed to bring a message of good tidings to the Arabs, the message of God through His angel Gabriel. He went back to his faithful wife exhausted in mind and body, but with his doubts laid at rest."

With the history of the spread of Mohammed's message we are not concerned in this volume. The fact that his own nearest of kin, those of his own household, believed in his divine mission, and held to him with unwavering faith during the many years of persecution that followed, is proof that Mohammed was indeed a man who had attained Illumination. If the condition of woman did not rise to the heights which we have a right to expect of the cosmic conscious man of the future, we must remember that eastern traditions have ever given woman an inferior place, and for the matter of that, St. Paul himself seems to have shared the then general belief in the inferiority of the female.

It is undeniable that Mohammed's domestic relations were of the most agreeable character; his kindness and consideration were without parallel;

his harem was made up for the most part of women who were refused and scorned by other men; widows of his friends. And the fact that the prophet was a man of the most abstemious habits argues the claim that compassion and kindness was the motive in most instances where he took to himself another and yet another wife.

However, the points which we are here dealing with, are those which directly relate to Mohammed's unquestioned illumination and the spirit of his utterances as contained in the Ku-ran, corroborate the experience of Buddha, of Jesus, and of all whose illumination has resulted in the establishment of a religious system.

Mohammed taught, first of all, the fact of the one God. "There is no God but Allah," was his cry, and, following the example, or at least paralleling the example of Jesus, he "destroyed their idols" and substituted the worship of one God, in place of the tribal deities, which were a constant source of disputation among the clans.

Compare the following, which is one of the five daily prayers of the faithful Muslim, with the Lord's prayer as used in Christian theology.

"In the name of God, the compassionate—the merciful.

Praise be to God, the Lord of the worlds,

The compassionate, the merciful.

The king of the day of judgment.

Thee do we worship and of Thee do we beg assistance.

Guide us in the right way,

The way of those to whom Thou hast been gracious,

Not of those with whom Thou art wroth, nor of the erring."

Mohammed never tired of telling his disciples and followers that God was "The Very-Forgiving." Among the many and sometimes strangely varied attributes of God (The Absolute), we find this characteristic most strongly and persistently dwelt upon—the ever ready forgiveness and mercifulness of God.

Every soorah of the Kur-an begins with the words: "In the name of God, the compassionate, the merciful," but, even as Jesus laid persistent emphasis upon the love of God, and yet up to very recent times, Christianity taught the fear and wrath of God, losing sight of the one great and important fact that God is love, and that love is God, so the Muslims overlooked the real message, and the greatness and the power and the fearfulness of God, is the incentive of the followers of the Illumined Mohammed.

The following extracts from the Kur-an are almost identical with many passages in the Holy Scriptures of the Christian, and are comparable with the sayings of the Lord Buddha.

"God. There is no God but He, the ever-living, the ever-subsisting. Slumber seizeth Him not nor sleep. To Him belongeth whatsoever is in the heavens and whatsoever is in the earth. Who is he that shall intercede with Him, save by His permission?"

The Muslim is a fatalist, but this may be due less to the teachings of the prophet than to the peculiar quality of the Arab nature, which makes him stake everything, even his own liberty upon the cast of a die.

The leading doctrine of the all-powerfulness of God seems to warrant the belief in fatalism—belief which offers a stumbling block to all theologians, all philosophers, all thinkers. If God is omnipotent, omnipresent, omniscient, how and where and in what manner can be explained the necessity of individual effort?

This problem is not at all clear to the western mind, and it is equally obscure to that of the East.

It is said of Mohammed that when asked concerning the doctrine of "fatalism" he would show more anger than at any other question that could be put to him. He found it impossible to explain that while all knowledge was God's, yet the individual was responsible for his own salvation, by virtue of his good deeds and words. Nevertheless, it is not unlikely that Mohammed possessed the key to this seeming riddle; but how could it be possible to speak in a language which was totally incomprehensible to them of this knowledge—the language of cosmic consciousness?

Like Jesus, who said: "Many things I have to tell you, but you can not bear (understand) them now," so, we may well believe that Mohammed was hard-pressed to find language comprehensible to his followers, in which to explain the all-knowingness and all-powerfulness of God, and at the same time, not have them fall into the error of the fatal doctrine of fatalism.

But throughout all his teachings Mohammed's chief concern seemed to be to draw his people away from their worship of idols, and to this end he laid constant and repeated emphasis upon the one-ness of God; the all-ness, the completeness of the one God; always adding "the Compassionate, the Loving."

This constant allusion to the all-ness of God is in line with all who have attained to cosmic consciousness. Nothing more impresses the illumined mind, than the fact that the universe is One—uni—(one)—verse—(song)—one glorious harmony when taken in its entirety, but when broken up and segregated, and set at variance, we find discord, even as the score of a grand operatic composition when played in unison makes perfect harmony but when incomplete, is nerve-racking.

Like all inspired teachers, Mohammed taught the end of the world of sense, and the coming of the day of judgment, and the final reign of peace and love. This may, of course, be interpreted literally, and applied to a life other than that which is to be lived on this planet, but it may also with equal logic be assumed that Mohammed foresaw the dawn of cosmic consciousness as a race-endowment, belonging to the inheritors of this sphere called earth. In either event the ultimate is the same, whether the one who suffers and attains, comes into his own in some plane or place in the heavens, or whether he becomes at-one with God, The Absolute Love and Power of the spheres, and "inherits the earth," in the days of the on-coming higher degree of consciousness, which we are here considering.

That Mohammed realized the nothingness of form and ritual, except it be accompanied by sincerity and understanding, is evident in the following:

"Your turning your faces in prayer, towards the East and the West, is not piety; but the pious is he who believeth in God, and the last day, and in the angels and in the Scripture; and the prophets, and who giveth money notwithstanding his love of it to relations and orphans, and to the needy and the son of the road, and to the askers for the freeing of slaves; and who performeth prayer and giveth the alms, and those who perform their covenant when they covenant; and the patient in adversity and affliction and the time of violence. These are they who have been true; and these are they who fear God."

Parallel with the doctrine taught by Buddha, and Jesus, is the advice to overcome evil with good. In our modern metaphysical language, we must dissolve the vibrations of hate, by the power of love, instead of opposing hate with hate, war with war, revenge with revenge.

Mohammed expressed this doctrine of non-resistance thus:

"Turn away evil by that which is better; and lo, he, between whom and thyself was enmity, shall become as though he were a warm friend."

"But none is endowed with this, except those who have been patient and none is endowed with it, except he who is greatly favored."

Mohammed meant by these words "he who is greatly favored," to explain that in order to see the wisdom and the glory of such conduct, one must have attained to spiritual consciousness. This was especially a new doctrine to the people to whom he was preaching, because it was considered cowardice to fail to resent a blow. Pride of family and birth was the strongest trait in the Arab nature.

In furtherance of this doing good to others, we find these words: "If ye are greeted with a greeting, then greet ye with a better greeting, or at least return it; verily. God taketh count of these things. If there be any under a difficulty wait until it be easy; but if ye remit it as alms, it will be better for you."

Mohammed here referred to debtors and creditors; as he was talking to traders, merchants, men who were constantly buying and selling, this admonition was in line with his teaching, which was to "do unto others that which you would that they do unto you."

In further compliance with his doctrine of doing good for good's sake Mohammed said: "If ye manifest alms, good will it be; but if ye conceal them and give them to the poor, it will be better for you; and it will expiate some of your sins."

Alms-giving, as an ostentatious display among church members, was here given its rightful place. It is well and good to give openly to organizations, but it is better to give to individuals who need it, secretly and quietly to give, without hope, or expectation, or desire for thanks, or for reward, to give for the love of giving, for the sole wish to make others happy. This desire to bestow upon others the happiness which has come to them, is a characteristic of the cosmic conscious man or woman.

It is comforting to know that Mohammed, like Buddha and The Man of Sorrows; and like Sri Ramakrishna, the saint of India, at length attained unto that peaceful calm that comes to one who has found the way of Illumination. It is doubtless impossible for the merely sense-conscious person to form any adequate idea of the inward urge; the agony of doubts and questionings; the imperative necessity such a one feels, to KNOW.

The sense-conscious person reads of the lives of these men and wonders why they could not be happy with the things of the world. The temptation that we are told came to Jesus in the garden, is typical of the state of transition from sense-consciousness to cosmic consciousness. The sense-conscious person regards the things of the senses as important. He is actuated by ambition or self-seeking or by love of physical comfort or by physical activity, to obtain the possessions of sense. To such as these, the agonies of mind; the physical hardships; the ever-ready forgiveness and the desire for peace and love of the Illuminate seem almost weaknesses. Therefore, they can not fully comprehend the satisfaction which comes to the one who has come into a realization of illumination, through the years of mental tribulation such as that endured by Mohammed and Jesus and Buddha.

We are told that the prophet repeatedly refuted the suggestion of his adoring followers that he was God himself come to earth.

"It is wonderful," says one of his commentators, "with his temptations, how great a humility was ever is, how little he assumed of all the godlike attributes men forced upon him. His whole life is one long argument for his loyalty to truth. He had but one answer for his worshippers, 'I am no more than a man; I am only human.' * * * He was sublimely confident of this single attribute that he was the messenger of the Lord of the daybreak, and that the words he spake came verily from him. He was fully persuaded that God had sent him to do a great work among his people in Arabia. Nervous to the verge of madness, subject to hysteria, given to wild dreaming in solitary places, his was a temperament that easily lends itself to religious enthusiasm."

While it may be argued that Mohammed did not possess cosmic consciousness in the degree of fullness which we find in the life of St. Paul, for example, we must take into consideration the temperament of the Arab, and the conditions under which he labored. But that he had attained a high degree of Illumination is beyond dispute. This fact is evidenced by the following salient points characteristic of cosmic consciousness: A fine sensitive, highly-strung organization; a deep and serious thoughtfulness, especially regarding the realities of life; an indifference to the call of personal ambition; love of solitude and the mental urge that demands to know the answer to life's riddle.

Following the time of illumination on Mount Hara we find Mohammed possessing a conviction of the truth of immortality and the goodness of God; we find him also with a wonderful power to draw people to him in loving service; and the irresistible desire to bring to his people the message of immortal life, and the necessity to look more to spiritual things than to the things of the flesh. Added to this, we find Mohammed changed from a shrinking, sensitive youth, given to much reflection and silent meditation, into a man with perfect confidence in his own mission and in his ultimate victory.

Chapter Twelve - Emanuel Swedenborg

While the Swedenborgians, as a religious sect, are not numerically sufficient to be reckoned among the world's great religions, it is yet a fact that the followers of the great Swedish seer and scientist hold a prominent place among the innumerable sects which the beginning of this century finds flourishing.

Swedenborg was born in Stockholm, in January, 1688, and lived to the advanced age of eighty-four years.

Swedenborg was well born; he was the son of a bishop of the Swedish church, and during his lifetime held many positions of honor. He was a friend and adviser of the king, and his expert knowledge of mining engineering gave him a place among the scientists of his age.

He was a voluminous writer, his early work being confined to the phases of materialistic science, notably on mines and metals, and later upon man, in his physiological aspect.

His "De Cerebro and Psychologia Rationales," published in his fifty-seventh year, showed a different Swedenborg from the one to whom his colleagues were accustomed to refer with much respect.

This book dealt with man, not as a product of brute creation, but as an evolutionary creature, having at least a possibility of divine origin. It is, however, his "Arcana Coelestia" upon which "The Church of the New Jerusalem" is founded; and it is this work which caused Swedenborg's friends and colleagues to determine that he had become insane. It is, in fact, only within very recent years, that the so-called scientific world has deigned to regard Swedenborg's revelations with any degree of serious and respectful attention.

Swedenborg's Illumination was not, like that of so many others, who have founded a new religion, a sudden influx of spiritual consciousness, but rather a gradual leading up to the inevitable goal, by virtue of serious thought, deep study, and a high order of mentality.

But that the Swedish seer received, in full measure, the blessing of cosmic consciousness, is beyond doubt.

Swedenborg's extremely simple habits of life; his freedom from any desire for display, or for those social advantages into which he was born; his gentleness and unassuming manner, of which much is written by his followers, all point to him as one upon whom the blessing might readily descend. Swedenborg was a vegetarian, but this seems not to be a necessary characteristic of those possessing illumination, although, when cosmic consciousness shall have become almost general, vegetarianism must inevitably come with it, as animal life will disappear from the earth.

Swedenborg, like many others who have perceived the cosmic light, evidently believed that he had been specially selected and consecrated for the work of the new church. That is, he took his illumination, not as an initiation into the higher degrees of cosmic truth, but as a special and personal revelation. This view characterizes those who founded a new, or a reformed religious system, while as a matter of truth, the light that comes is a part of the cosmic plan, and not, as Swedenborg and others imagine, as a personal revelation.

However, Swedenborg considered himself a direct instrument in the hands of God, and God is alluded to as a personality. He believed that his great mission was to disclose the true nature of the Bible, and to prove that it was actually the inspired word of God, having an esoteric meaning, which has wrongly been interpreted to apply to the creation of a material world, and to its history and its people, but that when understood, it explains clearly, the nature of God, and the nature of man, and their relation to each other. It should be remembered that at the time Swedenborg wrote his theological works, the church had fallen into rank materialism and superstition. That Swedenborg should have received his illumination, or revelation, direct from the Lord, only serves to prove that the mortal consciousness clothes the revelation with whatever personality appeals to it, as having authority.

Thus, the angel Gabriel was the dictator in the case of Mohammed, and the "Blessed Mother" of the Hindu reveals to them the vision of mukti. Swedenborg says of his vision: "God appeared to me and said, 'I am the Lord God, the Creator and Redeemer of the world. I have chosen thee to unfold the spiritual sense of the Holy Scriptures. I will myself dictate to thee what thou shalt write.'"

In "The True Christian Religion," published shortly before his death he says: "Since the Lord can not manifest Himself in person as has been shown, and yet He has foretold that He would come and establish a new church, which is the New Jerusalem, it follows that He is to do it, by means of a man, who is able not only to receive the doctrines of this church with his understanding, but also to publish them by the press. That the Lord has manifested Himself before me, His servant, and sent me on this office, and that, after this, He opened the sight of my spirit, and thus let me into the spiritual world, and gave me to see the heavens and the hells and also to speak with spirits and angels, and this now continually for many years, I testify in truth; and also that, from the first day of that call, I have not received anything that pertains to the doctrines of that church from my angel, but from the Lord alone, while I read the Word."

It is stated with great positiveness by Swedenborg's followers, and indeed, apparently by the seer himself, if we may take as authoritative, the translations of his works, that the revelations accorded to him covered a period of many years, whereas, we find in most instances of cosmic consciousness, the illumined ones have alluded to some specific time, as the great event, even while claiming that the effect of this illumination remains indefinitely—in fact, forms a part of a wider area of consciousness which is ever increasing.

But when we take the numerous instances of revelations, in which the devout ones firmly believe that they and they alone have been accorded the vision, we must realize that this phenomenon is impersonal, looked at as a favor to any one human being. By that we mean that Illumination comes to every soul who has earned it, just as mathematically as the sun seems to set, after the earth has made its hourly journey.

Perhaps this comparison is not as clear as to say: when the normal child has grown to manhood or womanhood, his consciousness has widened, beyond that of the infant; not excluding that of the infant but inclusive of all hitherto acquired knowledge. Without in any degree lessening the importance and the verity of Swedenborg's visions, it may be assumed that his record of these visions and their meaning has partaken more or less of the limitations of mortal mind.

Spiritual consciousness can not be set down in terms of sense. The external world symbolizes spiritual truths; each interpreter must of necessity weave into his interpretation and attempt at finite expression of these truths, something of his own mortal consciousness; and this "mortal mind" consciousness is bound to partake of the time and age, and conditions of environment of the person who has experienced the revelation.

Making due allowance, therefore, for the impossibility of exact expression of any spiritual illumination, we find in the revelation of Swedenborg exactly what we find in all who have attained to cosmic consciousness, namely, the absolute, confidential assurance of immortal life: the conviction that creation is under divine love and wisdom, administered by Cosmic Law and order, or Justice, and the final "redemption" (i.e., evolution), of all men. In his "Conjugal Love," Swedenborg touches upon the premise which we declare, as the foundation of all cosmic consciousness, namely the attainment of spiritual union with the "mate" which we believe to be inseparable from all creation; the reunited principle which we see expressed in the male and female, whether in plant, bird, animal, man, or angel; the "twain made one" which Jesus declared would be the sign manual of the coming of his kingdom; that is, the coming of cosmic consciousness—the kingdom of pure and perfect love upon earth as it is in the heavens.

In Corinthians (11: 12) we read:

"For as the woman is of the man so is the man also of the woman; for the woman is not without the man, nor the man without the woman in the Lord."

Which is to say, that in the attainment of cosmic consciousness (in the Lord), the "twain are made one," and immortality (i.e., immunity from reincarnation) is gained, because of this union. God is a bi-sexual Being. This fact is evidenced throughout all creation. To attain to immortality is to become as God. In this day and age of the world we have come into a realization of the Father-Mother idea of godhood, clearly and literally signifying the coming consciousness which is bi-sexual; male and female; perfect counterparts, or complements and through which alone, this earth can be made a "fit dwelling place for gods." This, too, is the message of the great seer Swedenborg, as it relates to love, as it is, when rightly understood and interpreted, of all who have felt the blessing of perfection, as exemplified in Illumination.

The fundamental points of Swedenborg's doctrine agree with those of all other Illumined ones, who have founded a system of worship; a "Way of Illumination" it may be called; or in whose name such systems have been formed. That is, he testified to:

A conviction of immortality;

A realization of absolute justice, whereby all souls shall finally come into cosmic consciousness.

An actual time when Christ (the cosmic illumination) shall come to earth.

A great and abiding love for and patience with the frailties of his sense-conscious fellow-beings;

A transcendent desire to bestow upon all men, the blessing of cosmic consciousness.

Few if any, have ever attained a full and complete realization of cosmic consciousness and remained in the physical body.

Those who have attained and retained the highest degree of this glimpse of the Paradise of the gods, find it practically impossible to describe or explain the sensations experienced, even though they are more convinced of the truth and the reality of this realm than of anything in the merely sense-conscious life.

Lastly, let us not lose sight of the all-important fact that no one system, creed, philosophy, or way of Illumination will answer for all types and degrees of men. "All things work together for good" to those who have the keenness of vision which precedes the full attainment of cosmic consciousness, as well as to those who have grasped its full significance.

The characteristic evidence of the potentiality of the present era of the world, is preeminently that of a desire for unity.

This desire is expressed in all the avenues of external life; its inner meaning is obscured by commercialism and self-interest, as in trusts and labor unions, but it is there nevertheless—the symbol of the inner urge toward unity in consciousness.

It is found in efforts at Communism, and in allied reform movements. It is particularly evident in the breaking down of church prejudices. In these days a Catholic priest and a Jewish rabbi find it not only expedient but mutually helpful, to unite in the work of municipal reform; in the abolition of child labor; in all things that will bring a better state of existence into daily human life.

The business man uses the phrase "let us get together on this" without knowing that he is expressing in terms of sense-consciousness, the urge of his own and his fellow beings' inner mind, which senses the fact of our unescapable Brotherhood.

All religious systems then, are good, as are all systems of philosophy. They are good because they are an attempt at bringing into the perspective of the mortal mind the reality of the soul and the soul life; the rule of the spiritually conscious ego over the physical body in order that we may now, in our present incarnation, claim immortality.

Chapter Thirteen - Modern Examples of Intellectual Cosmic Consciousness: Emerson; Tolstoi; Balzac

Passing over the ancient philosophers, Aristotle, Albertus Magnus, Plotinus, Marcus Aurelius, Pascal, Socrates, Plato, Aspasia, and others, all of whom had glimpsed, if not fully attained, cosmic consciousness, we come to a consideration of those cases in our own day and age, in which this superior consciousness has found expression through intellectual rather than through religious channels.

Of these latter, no more illustrious example can be cited than that of Ralph Waldo Emerson, the sage of Concord.

Emerson's nature was essentially religious, but his religion was not of the emotional quality so often found among enthusiasts, and which is almost always openly expressed when this religious enthusiasm is not balanced by intellectuality.

Analysis is frequently a foe to inspiration, but there are fare instances where the intellect is of such a penetrating and extraordinary quality that it carries the power of analysis into the unseen; in fact what we habitually term the unseen is a part of the visible to this type of mind. True intellect is a natural inheritance, a karmic attribute. The spurious kind is the result of education, and it invariably has its limitations. It stops short of the finer vibrations of consciousness and denies the reality of the inner life of man—which inner life constitutes the real to the character of intellect that penetrates beyond maya.

Of such a quality of intellect is that exemplified in Emerson. No mere tabulator of facts was he, but a dissector of the causes back of all the manifestation which he observed and studied and classified with the mental power of a god.

Nor is there lacking ample proof that Emerson experienced the phenomenon of the suddenness of cosmic consciousness—a degree of which he seems to have possessed from earliest youth.

In his essay on Nature, we find these words:

"Crossing a bare common in snow puddles at twilight, under a clouded sky, without having in my thoughts any occurrence of special good fortune, I have enjoyed a perfect exhilaration. I am glad to the brink of fear."

Emerson here alluded to a feeling of fear, which seems to have been experienced during a certain stage by many of those who have entered into cosmic consciousness. This fear is doubtless due to the presence in the human organism of what we may term the "animal instinct," which is an inheritance of the physical body. This same peculiar phenomenon oppresses almost everyone when coming into contact with a new and hitherto untried force.

A certain lady, who relates her experience in entering into the cosmic conscious state, says: "A certain part of me was unafraid, certain, secure and content, at the same time my mortal consciousness felt an almost overwhelming sense of fear."

Continuing, Emerson says:

"All mean egotism vanishes. I become a transparent eyeball; I am nothing; I see all; the currents of the Universal Being circulate through me; I am part or particle of God."

Emerson's powerful intellect would naturally describe such an experience in intellectual terms rather than, as in the instances heretofore recorded, in religious phraseology, but it must not be inferred that Emerson was less religious, in the true sense, than was Mohammed or St. Paul.

Emerson lived in an age when orthodoxy flourished, and he and his associates of the Transcendentalist cult, were regarded as non-religious, if not actually heretical. Therefore, it is that Emerson's keen intellect was brought to bear upon everything he encountered, not only in his own intimate experience but also in all that he read and heard, lest he be trapped into committing the error which he saw all about him, namely, of mistaking an accepted viewpoint as an article of actual faith. His way to the Great Light lay through the jungle of the mind, but he found the path clear and plain and he left a torchlight along the way.

Emerson fully recognized the illusory character of external life, and the eternal verity of the soul, as witness:

"If the red slayer thinks he slays,
Or if the slain thinks he is slain,
They know not well, the subtle ways,
I keep and pass and turn again."

Horrible as is war, because of the spirit of hate and destruction it embodies and keeps alive, yet the fact remains that man in his soul knows that he can neither slay nor be slain by the mere act of destroying the physical shell called the body. It is inconceivable that human beings would lend themselves to warfare, if they did not know, as a part of that area of supra-consciousness, that there is a something over which bullets have no power.

This fact, regarded as a more or less vague belief to the majority, becomes incontrovertible fact to the person who has entered cosmic consciousness. His view is reversed, and where he formerly looked from the sense-conscious plane forward into a possible spiritual plane, he now gazes back over the path from the spiritual heights and sees the winding road that led upward to the elevation, much as a traveller on the mountain top looks back and for the first time sees all of the devious trail over which he has, climbed to his present vantage point. During the journey there had been many times when he could only see the next step ahead, and nothing but his faith in the assurance of his fellow men who had attained the summit of that mountain, could ever have sustained him through the perils of the climb, but once on the heights, his backward view takes in the details of the journey and sees not "through a glass darkly," but in the clear light of achievement.

Such is the effect of cosmic consciousness to the one who has seen the light.

"One of the benefits of a college education," says Emerson, "is to show the boy its little avail."

Does this imply that an unlettered mind is desirable? Not necessarily, but there is a phase of intellectual culture that is detrimental while it lasts.

It is as though one were to choke up a perfectly flowing stream which yielded the moisture to fertile lands, by filling the bed of the stream with rocks and sticks.

The flow of the spiritual currents becomes clogged by the activities of the mind in its acquisition of mere knowledge, and before that knowledge has been turned into wisdom. The same truth is expressed in the aphorism "a little knowledge is a dangerous thing." It is dangerous because it chains the mind to the external things of life, whereas the totally unlettered (we do not use the term ignorant here) person will, if he have his heart filled with love, perceive the reality of spiritual things that transcend mere knowledge of the physical universe.

Beyond this plane of mortal mind-consciousness, which is fitly described as "dangerous," there is the wide open area of cosmic perception, which may lead ultimately to the limitless areas of cosmic consciousness. If, therefore, an education, whether acquired in or out of college, so whets the grain of the mind that it becomes keen and fine enough to realize that knowledge is valuable ONLY as it leads to real wisdom, then indeed it is a benefit; unless it does this, it is temporarily an obstruction.

Out of the lower into the higher vibration; out of sense-consciousness into cosmic consciousness; out of organization and limitations into freedom—the freedom of perfection, is the law and the purpose. This Emerson with his clearness of spiritual vision, saw, and this premise he subjected to the microscopic lens of his penetrating intellect. In his essay on Fate he says:

"Fate involves amelioration. No statement of the Universe can have any soundness which does not admit its ascending effort. The direction of the whole and of the parts is toward benefit. Behind every individual closes organization; before him opens liberty. * * * The Better; the Best. The first and worse races are dead. The second and imperfect races are dying out, or remain for the maturing of higher. In the latest race, in man, every generosity, every new perception, the love and praise he extorts from his fellows, are certificates of advance out of fate into freedom."

This phrase, "out of fate into freedom," may be read to mean, literally, out of the bondage of the sense-conscious life which entails rebirth and continued experience, into the light of Illumination which makes us free.

Further commenting, Emerson says:

"Liberation of the will from the sheaths and clogs of organization which he has outgrown is the end and aim of the world * * * The whole circle of animal life—tooth against tooth, devouring war, war for food, a yelp of pain and a grunt of triumph, until at last the whole menagerie, the whole chemical mass, is mellowed and refined for higher use * * *"

The sense of unity which is so inseparable from the cosmic conscious state, was always uppermost in Emerson's mind. Neither did he ever present as unity that state of consciousness that may be termed organization-consciousness—group-consciousness it is often called. He realized that the person who stands for Individualism is much more than apt to recognize his indissoluble relationship with the Cosmos. A perception of unity is a complement of Individualism.

That which, in modern metaphysical phraseology, is best termed "The Absolute," was expressed by Emerson as the Over-Soul, and this term meant something much greater, more unescapable than the anthropomorphic God of the church-goers. His assurance of unity with this Divine Spiritual Essence was perfect. It savors more of what is termed the religious view of life than of the philosophic, but we contend that in the coming era of the cosmic conscious man, all life will be religious, in the true sense, and that there will be no dividing line between philosophy and worship, because worship will consist of living the life of the spiritual man, and not in any set forms or rites. Bearing upon this we find Emerson saying:

"Not thanks, not prayer, seem quite the highest or truest name for our communion with the infinite—but glad and conspiring reception—reception that becomes giving in its turn as the receiver is only the All-Giver in part and in infancy. I cannot—nor can any man—speak precisely of things so sublime, but it seems to me the wit of man, his strength, his grace, and his tendency, his art, is the grace and the presence of God. It is beyond explanation. When all is said and done, the rapt saint is found the only logician. Not exhortation nor argument becomes our lips, but paeans of joy and praise. But not of adulation; we are too nearly related in the deep of the mind to that we honor. It is God in us that checks the language of petition by a grander thought. In the bottom of the heart it is said, 'I am and by me, O child, this fair body and world of thine stands and grows; I am, all things are mine; and all mine are thine.'"

We could quote passages from the essays ad infinitum, showing conclusively that the cosmic conscious plane had been attained and retained by this great philosopher—one of the first of the early part of the century, which has been prophesied as the beginning of the first faint lights of the Dawn, but enough has been offered for our present purpose, that of establishing the salient points of the cosmic conscious man or woman, which points are the complete assurance of the eternal verity and indestructibility of the soul; of its ultimate and inevitable victory over maya or the "wheel of causation"; and the joyousness and the sense of at-one-ness with the universe, which comes to the illumined one, bespeaking an unquenchable optimism and an utter destruction of the sense of sin—points which characterize all who have attained to this supra-conscious state of Being.

These points are all expressed repeatedly in all Emerson's utterances and mark him as one of the most illumined philosophers, as he was one of the greatest intellects of the last century, or of any other century.

Leo Tolstoi: Russian Philosopher

A strange, lonely and wonderful figure was Tolstoi, novelist, philosopher, socialist, artist and reformer.

Great souls are always lonely souls, estimated by sense-conscious humans. In the midst of the so-called pleasures and luxuries of the senses, a wise soul appears as barren of comfort as is a desert of foliage.

Without the divine optimism that comes from soul-consciousness, such a one could not endure the life of the body: without the absolute assurance that comes with cosmic consciousness, men like the late Count Tolstoi must needs die of soul-loneliness.

From early childhood up to the time of his Illumination Tolstoi indulged in seriousness of thought. Like Mohammed, great and overpowering desire to fathom the mystery of death took possession of him. He was ever haunted by an excessive dread of the "darkness of the grave," and in his essay, "Childhood," he describes with that wonderful realism, which characterizes all his works, the effect on a child's mind of seeing the face of his dead mother. This may be taken in a sense as biographical, although it is not probable that Tolstoi here alludes to the death of his own mother as she died when he was too young to have remembered. He describes the scene in the words of Irteniev:

"I could not believe that this was her face. I began to look at it more closely, and gradually discovered in it the familiar and beloved features. I shuddered with fear when I became sure that it was indeed she, but why were the closed eyes so fallen in? Why was she so terribly pale, and why was there a blackish mark under the clear skin on one cheek?"

A terror of death, and yet a haunting urge that compelled him to be forever thinking upon the mystery of it, is the dominant note in every line of Tolstoi's writings up to the time which he describes as "a change" that came over him.

For example, when Count Leo was in his 33d year, his brother Nicolai died. Leo was present at the bedside and described the scene with the utmost frankness regarding its effect upon his mind; and again we note that awful fear and hopeless questioning which characterizes the sense-conscious man whose intellect has been cultivated to the very edge of the line which separates the self-conscious life from the cosmic conscious.

This questioning, with the fear and dread and terror of death and of the "ceaseless round of births" and the cares and sorrows of existence was what drove Prince Siddhartha from his father's court and Mohammed into the mountains to meditate and pray until the answer came in the light of illumination.

It came to Tolstoi through the very intensity of his powers of reason and analysis; through the sword-like quality of mental urge—a much more sorrowful path than the one through the simple way of love and service and prayer.

His comments upon the death of his brother give us a vivid idea of the state of mind of the Tolstoi of that age:

"Never in my life has anything had such an effect upon me. He was right (referring to his brother's words) when he said to me there is nothing worse than death, and if you remember that death is the inevitable goal of all that lives, then it must be confessed that there is nothing poorer than life. Why should we be so careful when at the end of all things nothing remains of what was once Nicolai Tolstoi? Suddenly he started up and murmured in alarm: 'What is this?' He saw that he was passing into nothingness."

From the above it will be seen that the Tolstoi of those days was a materialist pure and simple. "He saw that he was passing into nothingness," he said of his brother, as though there could be no question as to the nothingness of the individual consciousness that he had known as Nicolai, his brother.

This soul-harrowing materialism haunted Tolstoi during all the years of his youth and early manhood, and threw him constantly into fits of melancholy and inner brooding. He could neither dismiss the subject from his mind, nor could he bring into the area of his mortal consciousness that serene contemplation and optimistic line of reasoning which marks all that Emerson wrote.

Tolstoi's morbid horror of decay and death was not in any sense due to a lack of physical courage. It was the inevitable repulsion of a strong and robust animalism of the body, coupled with a powerful mentality—both of which are barriers to the "still small voice" of the soul, through which alone comes the conviction of the nothingness of death.

A biographer says of Tolstoi:

"The fit of the fear of death which at the end of the seventies brought him to the verge of suicide, was not the first and apparently not the last and at any rate not the only one. He felt something like it fifteen years before when his brother Nicolai died. Then he fell ill and conjectured the presence of the complaint that killed his brother—consumption. He had constant pain in his chest and side. He had to go and try to cure himself in the Steppe by a course of koumiss, and did actually cure himself. Formerly these recurrent attacks of spiritual or physical weakness were cured in him, not by any mental or moral upheavals, but simply by his vitality, its exuberance and intoxication."

The birth of the new consciousness which came to Tolstoi a few years later, was born into existence through these terrible struggles and mental agonies, inevitable because of the very nature of his heredity and education and environment. Although as we know, he came of gentle-folk, there was much of the Russian peasant in Tolstoi's makeup. His organism, both as to physical and mental elements, was like a piece of solid iron, untempered by the refining processes of an inherent spirituality. His never-ceasing struggle for attainment of the degree of cosmic consciousness which he finally reached was wholly an intellectual struggle. He possessed such a power of analysis, such a depth of intellectual perception, that he must needs go on or go mad with the strain of the question unanswered.

To such a mind, the admonition to "never mind about those questions; don't think about them," fell upon dull ears. He could no more cease thinking upon the mysteries of life and death than he could cease respiration. Nor could he blindly trust. He must know. Nothing is more unescapable than the soul's urge toward freedom—and freedom can be won only by liberation from the bondage of illusion.

Tolstoi's friends and biographers agree that along about his forty-fifth year, a great moral and religious change took place. The whole trend of his thoughts turned from the mortal consciousness to that inner self whence issues the higher qualities of mankind.

From a man who, although he was a great writer and a Russian nobleman, was yet a man like others of his kind, influenced by traditionary ideas of class and outward appearance; a man of conventional habits and ideas; Tolstoi emerged a free soul. He shook off the illusion of historical life and culture, and stood upon free, moral ground, estimating himself and his fellows by means of an insight which ignores the world's conventions and despises the world's standards of success. In short, Tolstoi had received Illumination and henceforth should he reckoned among those of the new birth.

In his own words, written in 1879, this change is described:

"Five years ago a change took place in me. I began to experience at first times of mental vacuity, of cessation of life, as if I did not know why I was to live or what I was to do. These suspensions of life always found expression in the same problem, 'Why am I here?' and then 'What next?' I had lived and lived and gone on and on till I had drawn near a precipice; I saw clearly that before me there lay nothing but destruction. With all my might I endeavored to escape from this life. And suddenly I, a happy man, began to hide my bootlaces that I might not hang myself between the wardrobes in my room when undressing at night; and ceased to take a gun with me out shooting, so as to avoid temptation by these two means of freeing myself from this life. * * *

"I lived in this way (that is to say, in communion with the people) for two years; and a change took place in me. What befell me was that the life of our class—the wealthy and cultured—not only became repulsive to me, but lost all significance. All our actions, our judgments, science, and art itself, appeared to me in a new light. I realized that it was all self-indulgence, and that it was useless to look for any meaning in it. I hated myself and acknowledged the truth. Now it had all become clear to me."

From this time on, Tolstoi's life was that of one who had entered into cosmic consciousness, as we note the effects in others. Desire for solitude a taste for the simple, natural things of life, possessed him. The primitive peasants and their coarse but wholesome food appealed to him. It was not a penance that Tolstoi imposed upon himself, that caused him to abandon the life of a country gentleman for that of a hut in the woods. The penance would come to such a one from enforced living in the glare of the world's artificialities. Cosmic consciousness bestows above all things a taste for simplicity; it restores the normal condition of mankind, the intimacy with nature and the feeling of kinship with nature-children.

It is not our purpose here to enter into any detailed biography of these instances of cosmic consciousness. The point we wish to make is the fact that the birth of this new consciousness frequently comes through much mental travail and agonies of doubt, speculation and questioning; but that it is worth the price paid, however seemingly great, there can be no possible distrust.

Honore De Balzac

Balzac should head this chapter, if we were considering these philosophers in chronological order, as Balzac was born in 1799, preceding Emerson by a matter of four years. But Balzac's peculiar temperament, might almost be classed as a religious rather than strictly intellectual example of cosmic consciousness. Of the latter phase or expression of this "new" sense, as present-day writers frequently call it, Emerson is the most perfect example, because he was the most balanced; the most literary, in the strict interpretation of the word.

Balzac's place in literature is due far more to his wonderful spiritual insight, and his powerful imagination, than to his intellectuality, or to literary style. But that he was an almost complete case of cosmic consciousness is evident in all he wrote and in all he did. His life was absolutely consistent with the cosmic conscious man, living in a world where the race consciousness has not yet risen to the heights of the spiritually conscious life.

Bucke comments upon his decision against the state of matrimony, because, as Balzac himself declared, it would be an obstacle to the perfectibility of his interior senses, and to his flight through the spiritual worlds, and says: "When we consider the antagonistic attitude of so many of the great cases toward this relation (Gautama, Jesus, Paul, Whitman, etc.), there seems little doubt that anything like general possession of cosmic consciousness must abolish marriage as we know it to-day."

Balzac explains this seeming aversion to the marriage state as we know it to-day, in his two books, written during his early thirties, namely, Louis Lambert and Seraphita. "Louis Lambert" is regarded as in the nature of an autobiography, since Balzac, like his mouthpiece, Louis, viewed everything from an inner sense—from intuition, or the soul faculties, rather than from the standard of mere intellectual observation, analysis and synthesis. This inner sense, so real and so thoroughly understandable to those possessing it, is almost, if not quite, impossible of description to the complete comprehension of those who have no intimate relationship with this inner vision. To the person who views life from the inner sense, the soul sense (which is the approach to, and is included in, cosmic consciousness), the external or physical life is like a mirror reflecting, more or less inaccurately, the reality—the soul is the gazer, and the visible life is what he sees.

Balzac expresses this view in all he says and does. "All we are is in the soul," he says, and the perfection or the imperfection of what we externalize, depends upon the development of the soul.

It is this marvelously developed inner vision that makes marriage, on the sense-conscious plane, which is the plane upon which we know marriage as it is to-day, objectionable to Balzac.

His spirit had already united with its spiritual counterpart, and his soul sought the embodiment of that union in the flesh. This he did not find in the perfection and completeness which from his inner view he knew to exist.

Barriers of caste, or class; of time and space; of age; of race and color; of condition; may intervene between counterparts on the physical plane; nay, one may be manifesting in the physical body and the other have abandoned the body, but as there is neither time nor space nor condition to the spirit, this union may have been sought and found, and reflected to the mortal consciousness, in which case marriage with anything less than the one true counterpart would be unsatisfactory, if not altogether objectionable.

With this view in mind, Seraphita becomes as lucid a bit of reading as anything to be found in literature.

Seraphita is the perfected being—the god into which man is developing, or more properly speaking, unfolding, since man must unfold into that from which he started, but with consciousness added.

Everywhere, in ancient and modern mysticism, we find the assumption that God is dual—male and female. The old Hebrew word for God is plural—Elohim.

Humankind invariably and persistently, even though half-mockingly, alludes to man and wife as "one"; and men and women speak of each other, when married, as "my other half."

That which persists has a basis in fact, and symbolizes the perfect type. What we know of marriage as it is to-day, proves to us beyond the shadow of a doubt, that the man-made institution of marriage does not make man and woman one, nor insure that two halves of the same whole are united. The highest type of men and women to-day are at best but half-gods, but these are prophecies of the future race, "the man-god whom we await" as Emerson puts it. But that which we await is the man-woman-god, the Perfected Being, of whom Balzac writes in Seraphita.

It has been said that Madame Hanska, whom the author finally married only six months previous to his death, was the original of Seraphita, but it would seem that this great affection, tender and enduring as it was, partook far more of a beautiful friendship between two souls who knew and understood each other's needs, than it did of that blissful and ecstatic union of counterparts, which everywhere is described by those who have experienced it, as a sensation of melting or merging into the other's being.

Seraphita is the embodiment, in human form, of the idea expressed in the world-old belief in a perfected being; whose perfection was complete when the two halves of the one should have found each other.

The inference is very generally made that Balzac believed in and sought to express the idea of a bi-sexual individual—a personality who is complete in himself or herself as a person; one in which the intuitive, feminine principle and the reasoning, masculine principle had become perfectly balanced—in short, an androgynous human.

This idea is apparently further substantiated by the fact that Seraphita was loved by Minna, a beautiful young girl to whom Seraphita was always Seraphitus, an ideal lover; and by Wilfrid, to whom Seraphita represented his ideal of feminine loveliness, both in mind and body; a young girl possessing marvelous, almost miraculous, wisdom, but yet a woman with human passions and human virtues—his ideal of wifehood and motherhood.

But whatever the idea that Balzac intended to convey, whether, as is generally believed, Seraphita was an androgynous being, or whether she symbolized the perfection of soul-union, our contention is that this union is not a creation of the imagination, but the accomplishment of the plan of creation—the final goal of earthly pilgrimage; the raison d'etre of love itself.

One argument against the idea that Seraphita was intended to illustrate an androgynous being, rather than a perfected human, who had her spiritual mate, is found in the words in which she refused to marry Wilfrid, although Balzac makes it plainly evident that she was attracted to Wilfrid with a degree of sense-attraction, due to the fact that she was still living within the environment of the physical, and therefore subject to the illusions of the mortal, even while her spiritual consciousness was so fully developed as to enable her to perceive and realize the difference between an attraction that was based largely upon sense, and that which was of the soul.

Wilfrid says to her:

"Have you no soul that you are not seduced by the prospect of consoling a great man, who will sacrifice all to live with you in a little house by the border of a lake?"

"But," answers Seraphita, "I am loved with a love without bounds."

And when Wilfrid with insane anger and jealousy asked who it was whom Seraphita loved and who loved her, she answered "God."

At another time, when Minna, to whom she had often spoken in veiled terms of a mysterious being who loved her and whom she loved, asked her who this person was, she answered:

"I can love nothing here on earth."

"What dost thou love then?" asked Minna.

"Heaven" was the reply.

This obscurity and uncertainty as to what manner of love it was that absorbed Seraphita, and who was the object of it, could not have been possible had it been the usual devotion of the religeuse.

Seraphita, whose consciousness extended far beyond that of the people about her, could not have explained to her friends that the invisible realms were as real to her as the visible universe was to those with only sense-consciousness. It was impossible to explain to them that she had found and knew her mate, even though she had not met him in the physical body.

To Wilfrid she said she loved "God." To Minna she used the term "Heaven," and when Minna questioned: "But art thou worthy of heaven when thou despisest the creatures of God?" Seraphita answered:

"Couldst thou love two beings at once? Would a lover be a lover if he did not fill the heart? Should he not be the first, the last, the only one? She who loves will she not quit the world for her lover? Her entire family becomes a memory; she has no longer a relative. The lover! she has given him her whole soul. If she has kept a fraction of it, she does not love. To love feebly, is that to love? The word of the lover makes all her joy, and quivers in her veins like a purple deeper than blood; his glance is a light which penetrates her; she dissolves in him; there, where he is, all is beautiful; he is warmth to the soul: he irradiates everything; near him could one know cold or night? He is never absent; he is ever within us; we think in him, to him, for him. Minna, that is the-way I love."

And when Minna, like Wilfrid, "seized by a devouring jealousy," demanded to know "whom?" Seraphita answered, "God." This she did because the one whom she loved became her God. We are told that "love makes gods of men." Perfect love, the love of those who are spiritual-mates—soul-mates—the "man-woman-god whom we await," becomes an immortal: and immortals are gods.

Moreover if Seraphita had intended to teach the love of the religious devotee to The Absolute instead of a perfected sex-love, she would not have pointed out to both Wilfrid and Minna that which she, in her superior vision, her supra-consciousness, perceived, namely, that Wilfrid and Minna were really intended for spiritual mates, and that what they each saw in her was really a prophecy of their own perfected and spiritualized love.

The subject is one that is positively incomprehensible and unexplainable to the average mind. All mystic literature, when read with the eyes of understanding, exalts and spiritualizes sex. The latter day degeneration of sex is the "trail of the serpent," which Woman is to crush with her heel. And Woman is crushing it to-day, although to the superficial observer, who sees only surface conditions, it would appear as though Woman had fallen from her high estate, to take her place on a footing with man. This view is the exoteric, and not the esoteric, one.

They who have ears hear the inner voice, and they who have eyes see with the inner sight. The mystery of sex is the eternal mystery which each must solve for himself before he can comprehend it, and when solved eliminates all sense of sin and shame; brings Illumination in which everything is made clear and makes man-woman immortal—a god.

Swedenborg's theory of Heaven as a never-ending honeymoon in which spiritually-mated humans dwell, has been denounced by many as "shocking" to a refined and sensitive mind. But this idea is shocking only because even the most advanced minds are seldom Illumined, their advancement being along the lines of intellectual research and acquired knowledge, which, as we have previously explained, is not synonymous with interior wisdom.

The illumined mind is bound to find in the eternal and ever-present fact of sex, the key to the mysteries—the password to immortal godhood.

The subject is one that cannot be set forth in printed words; this fact is, indeed, the very Plan of Illumination. It cannot be taught. It must be found. Only those who have glimpsed its truth can even imperfectly point the way in which it may be discovered. No teacher can guarantee it. It is the most evanescent, the most delicate, the most indescribable thing in the Cosmos. It is therefore the most readily misinterpreted and misunderstood.

Balzac doubtless understood, not as a matter of perception of a truth but as an experience, and this fact, if no other, marks him as one having a very high degree of cosmic consciousness.

Seraphita called herself a "Specialist." When Minna inquired how it was that Seraphitus could read the souls of men, the answer was:

"I have the gift of Specialism. Specialism is an inward sight that can penetrate all things; you will understand its full meaning only through comparison. In the great cities of Europe works are produced by which the human hand seeks to represent the effects of the moral nature as well as those of the physical nature, as well as those of the ideas in marble. The sculptor acts on the stone; he fashions it; he puts a realm of ideas into it. There are statues which the hand of man has endowed with the faculty of representing the whole noble side of humanity, or the evil side of it; most men see in such marbles a human figure and nothing more; a few older men, a little higher in the scale of being, perceive a fraction of the thoughts expressed in the statue; but the Initiates in the secrets of art are of the same intellect as the sculptor; they see in his work the whole universe of thought. Such persons are in themselves the principles of art; they bear within them a mirror which reflects nature in her slightest manifestations. Well, so it is with me; I have within me a mirror before which the moral nature, with its causes and its effects, appears and is reflected. Entering thus into the consciousness of others I am able to divine both the future and the past * * * though what I have said does not define the gift of Specialism, for to conceive the nature of that gift we must possess it."

This describes in terms similar to those employed by others who possess cosmic consciousness, the results of this inner light, which Seraphita calls a "mirror."

And yet, with this seemingly exhaustive and lucid exposition of the effects of Illumination, Seraphita declares that "to conceive the nature of this gift we must possess it."

Balzac further comments upon what he terms this gift of Specialism, which is cosmic consciousness or illumination, thus:

"The specialist is necessarily the loftiest expression of man—the link which connects the visible to the superior worlds. He acts, he sees, he feels through his inner being. The abstractive thinks. The instinctive simply acts. Hence three degrees for man. As an instinctive he is below the level; as an abstractive he attains it; as a specialist he rises above it. Specialism opens to man his true career; the Infinite dawns upon him—he catches a glimpse of his destiny."

The merely sense-conscious man is the man-animal; the abstractive man is the average man and woman in the world to-day—the human who is evolving out of the mental into the spiritual consciousness. The specialist is the cosmic conscious one, the one who "catches a glimpse of his destiny."

Balzac, in company with all who attain cosmic consciousness, had a great capacity for suffering; and this soul-loneliness became crystalized into spiritual wisdom, which he expressed in the words and in the manner most likely to be accepted by the world.

How else can that divine union to which we are heirs and for which we are either blindly, consciously, or supra-consciously, striving, be described and exploited without danger of defilement and degeneracy, save and except by the phrase "unity with God"?

All mystics have found it necessary to veil the "secret of secrets," lest the unworthy (because unready) defile it with his gaze, even as the sinful devotee prostrates himself hiding his face, while the priest raises the chalice containing the holy eucharist in the ceremony of the mass.

Chapter Fourteen - Illumination as Expressed in the Poetical Temperament

Poetry is the natural language of cosmic consciousness. "The music of the spheres" is a literal expression, as all who have ever glimpsed the beauties of the spiritual realms will testify.

"Poets are the trumpets which sing to battle. Poets are the unacknowledged legislators of the world," said Shelley.

Not that all poets are aware, in their mortal consciousness, of their divine mission, or of their spiritual glimpses.

The outer mind, the mortal or carnal mind—that part of our organism whose office it is to take care of the physical body, for its preservation and its well-being, may be so dominant as, to hold in bondage the atman, but it can not utterly silence its voice.

Thus the true poet is also a seer; a prophet; a spiritually-conscious being, for such time, or during such phases of inspiration, as he becomes imbued with the spirit of poetry.

A person who writes rhymes is not necessarily a poet. So, too, there are poets who do not express their inspirations according to the rules of metre and syntax.

Between that which Balzac tabulated as the "abstractive" type of human evolvement and that which is fully cosmic in consciousness, there are many and diverse degrees of the higher faculties; but the poet always expresses some one of these degrees of the higher consciousness; indeed some poets are of that versatile nature that they run the entire gamut of the emotional nature, now descending to the ordinary normal consciousness which takes account only of the personal self; again ascending to the heights of the impersonal fearlessness and unassailable confidence that is the heritage of those who have reached the full stature of the "man-god whom we await"—the cosmic conscious race that is to be.

All commentators upon modern instances of Illumination unite in regarding Walt Whitman as one of the most, if not the most, perfect example of whom we have any record of cosmic consciousness and its sublime effects upon the character and personality of the illumined one.

Whitman is a sublime type for reasons which are of first importance in their relation to character as viewed from the ideals of the cosmic conscious race-to-be.

Moralists have criticized Whitman as immoral; religionists have deplored his lack of a religious creed; literary critics have denied his claim to high rank in the world of literature; but Walt Whitman is unquestionably without a peer in the roundness of his genius; in the simplicity of his soul; in the catholicity of his sympathy; in the perfect poise and self-control and imperturbability of his kindness. His biographers agree as to his never-failing good nature. He was without any of those fits of unrest and temperamental eccentricities which are supposed to be the "sign manual" of the child of the poetic muse.

In Whitman it would seem that all those petty prejudices against any nationality or class of men, were entirely absent. He exalted the common-place, not as a pose, nor because he had given himself to that task, but because to him there was no common-place. In the cosmic perception of the universe, everything is exalted to the plane of fitness. As to the pure all things are pure, so to the one who is steeped in the sublimity of Divine Illumination, there is no high or low, no good or bad, no white or black, or rich or poor; all—all is a part of the plan, and, in its place in cosmic evolution, it fits.

Whitman cries:

"All! all! Let others ignore what they may, I make the poem of evil also, I commemorate that part also; I am myself just as much evil as good, and my nation is, and I say there, is in fact no evil."

Compared to the religious aspect of cosmic consciousness in which, previous to the time of Illumination, the devotee had striven to rise to spiritual heights through disdaining the flesh, this note of Whitman's is a new note—the nothingness of evil as such; the righteousness of the flesh and the holiness of earthly, or human, love, bespeaks the prophet of the New Dispensation; the time hinted of by Jesus, the Master, when he said, "when the twain shall be one and the outside as the inside," as a sign and symbol of the blessed time to come when the kingdom he spoke of (not his personal kingdom, but the kingdom which he represented, the kingdom of Love), should come upon earth.

Whitman's illumination is essentially poetic; not that it is not also intellectual and moral; but after his experience—at least an experience more notable than any hitherto recorded by him, in or about his thirty-fifth year—we find his conversation invariably reflecting the beauty and poetical imagery of his mind. He may be said to have lived and moved and had his being in a state of blissful unconsciousness of anything unclean or impure, or unnatural.

This absence of consciousness of evil is in no wise synonymous with a type of person who exalts his undeveloped animal tendencies under the guise of liberation from a sense of sin. Neither is this discrimination easy of attainment to any but those who realize in their own hearts the very distinct difference between the nothingness of sin and the pretended acceptance of perversions as purity.

While we are on this point we must again emphasize the truth that cosmic consciousness cannot be gained by prescription; there is no royal road to mukti. Liberation from the lower manas can not be bought or sold, it can not be explained or comprehended, save by those to whom the attainment of such a state is at least possible if not probable.

Illustrative of his sense of unity with all life (one of the most salient characteristics of the fully cosmic conscious man), are these lines of Whitman's:

"Voyaging to every port, to dicker and adventure;
Hurrying with the modern crowd, as eager and fickle as any;
Hot toward one I hate, ready in my madness to knife him;
Solitary at midnight in my back yard, my thoughts gone from me a long while;
Walking the hills of Judea, with the beautiful gentle God by my side;
Speeding through space—speeding through Heaven and the stars."

Oriental mysticism tells us that one of the attributes of the liberated one is the power to read the hearts and souls of all men; to feel what they feel; and to so unite with them in consciousness that we are for the time being the very person or thing we contemplate. If this be indeed the test of godhood, Whitman expresses it in every line:

"The disdain and calmness of olden martyrs;
The mother condemned for a witch, burnt with dry wood, her children gazing on;
The hounded slave that flags in the race, leans by the fence, blowing, covered with sweat;
The twinges that sting like needles his legs and neck—the murderous buckshot and the bullets;
All these I feel, or am."

Seeking to express the sense of knowing and especially of feeling, and the bigness and broadness of life, the scorn of petty aims and strife; in short, that interior perception which Illumination brings, he says:

"Have you reckoned a thousand acres much? have you reckoned the earth

much?
Have you practised so long to learn to read?
Have you felt so proud to get at the meaning of poems?
Stop this day and night with me and you shall possess the origin of all poems;
You shall possess the good of the earth and sun—there are millions of suns left;
You shall no longer take things at second or third hand, nor look through the eyes of the dead, nor feed on the spectres in books;
You shall not look through my eyes either, nor take things from me;
You shall listen to all sides, and filter them from yourself.
I have heard what the talkers were talking, the talk of the beginning and the end;
But I do not talk of the beginning nor the end.

* * * * *

"There was never any more inception than there is now;
Nor any more youth or age than there is now;
And will never be any more perfection than there is now,
Nor any more heaven or hell than there is now."

A perception of eternity as an ever-present reality is one of the characteristic signs of the inception of the new birth.

Birth and death become nothing more nor yet less, than events in the procedure of eternal life; age becomes merely a graduation garment; God and heaven are not separated from us by any reality; they become every-day facts.

Whitman tells of the annihilation of any sense of separateness from his soul side, in the following words:

"Clear and sweet is my soul, and clear and sweet is all that is not my soul."

He did not confound his mortal consciousness, the lower manas, with the higher—the soul; neither did he recognize an impassable gulf between them.

While admittedly ascending to the higher consciousness from the lower, Whitman refused to follow the example of the saints and sages of old, and mortify or despise the lower self—the manifestation. He had indeed struck the balance; he recognized his dual nature, each in its rightful place and with its rightful possessions, and refused to abase either "I am" to the other. He literally "rendered unto Cæsar the things that are Cæsar's," by claiming for the flesh the purity and the cleanliness of God's handiwork.

In Whitman, too, we find an almost perfect realization of immortality and of blissfulness of life and the complete harmony and unity of his soul with all there is. Following closely upon the experience that seems to have been the most vivid of the many instances of illumination which he enjoyed throughout a long life, he wrote the following lines, indicative of the emotions immediately associated with the influx of illumination:

"Swiftly arose and spread around me, the peace and joy and knowledge that

pass all the art and argument of earth;
And I know that the hand of God is the elder hand of my own,
And I know that the spirit of God is the eldest brother of my own,
And that all the men ever born are also my brothers, and the women my sisters and lovers,
And that a kelson of creation is love."

In lines written in 1860, about seven years after the first vivid instance of the experience of illumination which afterward became oft-recurrent, Whitman speaks of what he calls "Perfections," and from what he writes we may assume that he referred to those possessing cosmic consciousness, and the practical impossibility of describing this peculiarity and accounting for the alteration it makes in character and outlook.

Says Whitman:

"Only themselves understand themselves, and the like of themselves,
As souls only understand souls."

It has been pointed out that Whitman more perfectly illustrates the type of the coming man—the cosmic conscious race, because Whitman's illumination seems to have come without the terrible agonies of doubt and prayer and mortification of the flesh, which characterize so many of those saints and sages of whom we read in sacred literature. But it must not be inferred from this that Whitman's life was devoid of suffering.

A biographer says of him:

"He has loved the earth, sun, animals; despised riches, given alms to every one that asked; stood up for the stupid and crazy; devoted his income and labor to others; according to the command of the divine voice; and was impelled by the divine impulse; and now for reward he is poor, despised, sick, paralyzed, neglected, dying. His message to men, to the delivery of which he devoted his life, which has been dearer in his eyes (for man's sake) than wife, children, life itself, is unread, or scoffed and jeered at. What shall he say to God? He says that God knows him through and through, and that he is willing to leave himself in God's hands."

But above and beyond all this, is the sense of oneness with all who suffer which is ever a heritage of the cosmic conscious one, even while he is, at the same time, the recipient of states of bliss and certainty of immortality, and melting soul-love, incomprehensible and indescribable to the non-initiate. Whitman's calm and poise was not that of the ice-encrusted egotist. It is the poise of the perfectly balanced man-god equally aware of his human and his divine attributes; and justly estimating both; nor drawing too fine a line between.

"I embody all presence outlawed or suffering;
See myself in prison, shaped like another man,
And feel the dull unintermitted pain.

* * * * *

"For me the keepers of convicts shoulder their carbines and keep watch;

It is I left out in the morning, and barr'd at night.
Not a mutineer walks handcuffed to jail, but I am handcuffed and walk by his side;

* * * * *

"Not a youngster is taken for larceny, but I go up too, and am tried and sentenced.
Not a cholera patient lies at the last gasp but I also lie at the last gasp;
My face is ash-colored—my sinews gnarl—away from me people retreat.

* * * * *

"Askers embody themselves in me, and I am embodied in them;
I project my hat, sit shame-faced and beg."

If any one imagines that Whitman was not a religious man, let him read the following:
"I say that no man has ever yet been half devout enough;
None has ever yet adored or worshipped half enough;
None has begun to think how divine he himself is, and how certain the future is."

There is a sublime confidence and worship in these words which belittles the churchman's hope and prayer that God may be good to him and bless him with a future life. Whitman's philosophy, less specific as to method, is assuredly more certain, more faithful in effect. Whitman had the experience of being immersed in a sea of light and love, so frequently a phenomenon of Illumination; he retained throughout all his life a complete and perfect assurance of immortality.

His sense of union with and relationship to all living things was as much a part of him as the color of his eyes and hair; he did not have to remind himself of it, as a religious duty.

He experienced a keen joy in nature and in the innocent, childlike pleasures of everyday things, and at the same time possessed a splendid intellect.

All consciousness of sin or evil had been erased from his mind and actually had no place in his life.

Alfred, Lord Tennyson

In the case of Lord Tennyson, we have a definite recognition of two distinct states of consciousness, finally culminating in a clear experience of cosmic consciousness; this experience was so positive as to leave no doubt or indecision in his mind regarding the reality of the spiritual, and the illusory character of the external life.

In truth Tennyson had so fixed his consciousness in the spiritual rather than in the external, that he looked out from that inner self, as through the windows of a house; he was prepared, as he said, to believe that his body was but an imaginary symbol of himself, but nothing and no one could persuade him that the real Tennyson, the I am consciousness of being which was he, was other than spiritual, eternal, undying.

Like so many others, notably Whitman, who have realized a more or less full degree of cosmic consciousness, Tennyson was deeply and reverently religious, although not partisanly connected with church work. Tennyson's early boyhood was marked by experiences which usually befall persons of the psychic temperament. As he himself described these states of consciousness, they were moments in which the ego transcended the limits of self consciousness and entered the limitless realm of spirit.

They do not tabulate with the ordinary trance condition of the spiritualistic medium, who subjects his own self consciousness to a "control," although Tennyson always believed that the best of his writings were inspired by, and written under "the direct influence of higher intelligences, of whose presence he was distinctly conscious. He felt them near him and his mind was impressed by their ideas."

The point which we emphasize is that these peculiar states of consciousness are not synonymous with the western idea of trance as seen in mediumship, although Tennyson uses the term "trance" in describing them.

He says:

"A kind of walking trance I have frequently had, quite up from boyhood, when I have been all alone. This has often come upon me through repeating my own name to myself silently until all at once, as it were, out of the intensity of the consciousness of individuality, the individuality itself seemed to dissolve and fade into boundless being."

It is a fact that children of a peculiarly sensitive or psychic temperament seem to have strange ideas regarding the name by which they are called, and not infrequently become confused and filled with an inexplicable wonderment at the sound of their own name. This phenomenon is much less rare than is generally known.

In Tennyson's "Ancient Sage" this experience of entering into cosmic consciousness is thus described:

> "More than once when I
> Sat all alone, revolving in myself,
> The word that is the symbol of myself,
> The mortal limit of the Self was loosed,
> And passed into the nameless, as a cloud
> Melts into heaven. I touched my limbs; the limbs
> Were strange, not mine; and yet no shade of doubt,
> But utter clearness, and thro' loss of self
> The gain of such large life as matched with ours
> Were sun to spark—unshadowable in words.
> Themselves but shadows of a shadow-world."

Tennyson's illumination is certain, clearly defined, distinct and characteristic, although his poems are much less cosmic than those of Whitman and of many others. There is, however, in the above, all that is descriptive of that state of consciousness which accompanies liberation from the illusion—the enchantment of the merely mortal existence.

Words are, as Tennyson fitly says, but "shadows of a shadow-world"; how then may we hope to define in terms comprehensible to sense-consciousness only, emotions and experiences which involve loss of self, and at the same time gain of the Self?

Tennyson's frequent excursions into the realm of spiritual consciousness while still a child, bears out our contention that many children not infrequently have this experience, and either through reserve or from lack of ability to explain it, keep the matter to themselves; generally losing or "outgrowing" the tendency as they enter the activities of school life, and the mortal mind becomes dominant in them. This is especially true of the rising generation, and we personally know several clearly defined instances which have been reported to us, during conversations upon the theme of cosmic consciousness.

Yone Noguchi

Any one who has ever had the good fortune to read a little book of verse entitled "From the Eastern Seas," by Yone Noguchi, a young Japanese, will at once pronounce them a beautiful and perhaps perfect example of verse that may be correctly labeled "cosmic."

Noguchi was under nineteen years of age when he penned these verses, but they are thoughts and expressions possible only to one who lives the greater part of his life within the illumination of the cosmic sense. They are so delicate as to have little, if any, of the mortal in them.

It is also significant that Noguchi in these later years (he is now only a little past thirty), does not reproduce this cosmic atmosphere in his writings to such an extent, due no doubt to the fact that his daily occupation (that of Professor of Languages in the Imperial College of Tokio), compels his outer attention, excluding the fullness of the inner vision.

The following lines, are perfect as an exposition of spiritual consciousness in which the lesser self has become submerged:

"Underneath the shade of the trees, myself passed into somewhere as a cloud.
I see my soul floating upon the face of the deep, nay the faceless face of the deepless deep—
Ah, the seas of loneliness.
The silence-waving waters, ever shoreless, bottomless, colorless, have no shadow of my passing soul.
I, without wisdom, without foolishness, without goodness, without badness—am like God, a negative god at least."

The almost perpetual state of spiritual consciousness in which the young poet lived at this time is apparent in the following lines:

> "When I am lost in the deep body of the mist on a hill,
> The universe seems built with me as its pillar.
> Am I the god upon the face of the deep, nay—
> The deepless deepness in the beginning?"

And the following, possible of comprehension only to one who has glimpsed the eternal verity of man's spiritual reality, and the shadow-like quality of the external; could have been written only by one freed from the bonds of illusion:

> "The mystic silence of the moon,
> Gradually revived in me immortality;
> The sorrow that gently stirred
> Was melancholy-sweet; sorrow is higher
> Far than joy, the sweetest sorrow is supreme
> Amid all the passions. I had
> No sorrow of mortal heart: my sorrow
> Was one given before the human sorrows
> Were given me. Mortal speech died
> From me: my speech was one spoken before
> God bestowed on me human speech.
> There is nothing like the moon-night
> When I, parted from the voice of the city,
> Drink deep of Infinity with peace
> From another, a stranger sphere. There is nothing
> Like the moon-night when the rich, noble stars
> And maiden roses interchange their long looks of love.
> When I raise my face from the land of loss
> Unto the golden air, and calmly learn
> How perfect it is to grow still as a star.
> There is nothing like the moon-night
> When I walk upon the freshest dews,
> And amid the warmest breezes,
> With all the thought of God
> And all the bliss of man, as Adam
> Not yet driven from Eden, and to whom
> Eve was not yet born. What a bird
> Dreams in the moonlight is my dream:
> What a rose sings is my song."

The true poet does not need individual experiences of either sorrow or of joy. His spirit is so attuned to the song of the universe; so sympathetic with the moans of earthly trials, that every vibration from the heart of the universe reaches him; stabs him with its sorrow, or irradiates his being with joy.

Jesus is fitly portrayed to us as "The Man of Sorrows"; even while we recognize him as a self-conscious son of God—an immortal being fully aware of his escape from enchantment, and his heirship to Paradise.

Cosmic consciousness bestows a bliss that is past all words to describe and it also quickens the sympathies and attunes the soul to the vibrations of the heart-cries of the struggling evolving ones who are still travailing in the pains of the new birth. We must be willing to endure the suffering in order that we may realize the joy; not because joy is the reward for suffering, but because it is only by losing sight of the personal self that we become aware of that inner Self which is immortal and blissful; and when we become aware of the reality of that inner Self, we know that we are united with the all, and must feel with all.

It would be impossible in one volume to enumerate all the poets who have given evidence of supra-consciousness. As has been previously pointed out, all true poets are at least temporarily aware of their dual nature—rather, one should say, the dual phases of their consciousness. Many, perhaps, do not function beyond the higher planes of the psychic vibrations, but even these are aware of the reality of the soul, and the illusion of the sense-conscious, mortal life.

Dante; the Brownings; Shelley; Swinbourne; Goethe; Milton; Keats; Rosetti; Shakespeare; Pope; Lowell—where should we stop, did we essay to draw a line?

Wordsworth

Wordsworth, the poet of Nature has given us in his own words, so clearly cut an outline of his Illumination, that we can not resist recording here the salient points which mark his experience as that of cosmic consciousness, transcending the more frequent phenomenon of soul-consciousness and its psychic functions.

Wordsworth's Ode to immortality epitomizes the lesson of the Yoga sutras—out of The Absolute we come, and return to immortal bliss with consciousness added. Wordsworth also affords an excellent example of our contention that cosmic consciousness does not come to us at any specific age or time. Wordsworth distinctly says that as a child he possessed this faculty, as for example his oft-repeated words, both in conversation and in his biography:

"Nothing was more difficult for me in childhood than to admit the notion of death, as a state applicable to my own being. It was not so much from feelings of animal vivacity that my difficulty came, as from a sense of the indomitableness of the spirit within me. I used to brood over the stories of Enoch and Elijah, and almost to persuade myself that, whatever might become of others, I should be translated, in something of the same way, to heaven. With a feeling congenial to this, I was often unable to think of external things as having external existence, and I communed with all that I saw as something not apart from, but inherent in, my own immaterial nature. Many times while going to school have I grasped at a wall or tree, to recall myself from this abyss of idealism to the reality."

In later life, Wordsworth lost the realization of this supra-consciousness, in what a commentator calls a "fever of rationalism"; but the power of that wonderful spiritual vision, pronounced in his youth, could not be utterly lost and soon after he reached his thirtieth year, he again becomes the spiritual poet, fully conscious of his higher nature—the cosmic conscious self.

William Sharp—"Fiona Macleod"

A pronounced instance of the two phases of consciousness, is that of the late William Sharp, one of the best known writers of the modern English school.

It was not until after the death of William Sharp, that the secret of this dual personality was given to the public, although a few of his most intimates had known it for several years. In the "Memoirs" compiled by Elizabeth Sharp, wife of the writer, we find the following:

"The life of William Sharp divides itself naturally into two halves: the first ends with the publication by William Sharp of 'Vistas,' and the second begins with 'Pharais,' the first book signed Fiona Macleod."

In these memoirs, the point is made obvious that Fiona Macleod is not merely a nom de plume; neither is she an obsessing personality; a guide or "control," as the Spiritualists know that phenomenon. Fiona Macleod, always referred to by William Sharp as "she," is his own higher Self—the cosmic consciousness of the spiritual man which was so nearly balanced in the personality of William Sharp as to appear to the casual observer as another person.

It is said that the identity of Fiona Macleod, as expressed in the manuscript put out under that name, was seldom suspected to be that of William Sharp, so different was the style and the tone of the work of these two phases of the same personality.

In this connection it may be well to quote his wife's opinion regarding the two phases of personality, answering the belief of Yeats the Irish poet that he believed William Sharp to be the most extraordinary psychic he ever encountered and saying that Fiona Macleod was evidently a distinct personality. In the Memoirs, Mrs. Sharp comments upon this and says:

"It is true, as I have said, that William Sharp seemed a different person when the Fiona mood was on him; but that he had no recollection of what he said in that mood was not the case—the psychic visionary power belonged exclusively to neither; it influenced both and was dictated by laws he did not understand."

Mrs. Sharp refers to William Sharp and Fiona, as two persons, saying that "it influenced both," but both sides of his personality rather than both personalities, is what she claims. In further explanation she writes:

"I remember from early days how he would speak of the momentary curious 'dazzle in the brain,' which preceded the falling away of all material things and precluded some inner vision of great beauty, or great presences, or some symbolic import—that would pass as rapidly as it came. I have been beside him when he has been in trance and I have felt the room throb with heightened vibration."

One of the "dream-visions" which William Sharp experienced shortly before his last illness, is headed "Elemental Symbolism," and was recorded by him in these beautiful words:

"I saw Self, or Life, symbolized all about me as a limitless, fathomless and lonely sea. I took a handful and threw it into the grey silence of ocean air, and it returned at once as a swift and potent flame, a red fire crested with brown sunrise, rushing from between the lips of sky and sea to the sound as of innumerable trumpets."

"In another dream he visited a land where there was no more war, where all men and women were equal; where humans, birds and beasts were no longer at enmity, or preyed on one another. And he was told that the young men of the land had to serve two years as missionaries to those who lived at the uttermost boundaries. 'To what end?' he asked. 'To cast out fear, our last enemy.' In the house of his host he was struck by the beauty of a framed painting that seemed to vibrate with rich colors. 'Who painted that?' he asked. His host smiled, 'We have long since ceased to use brushes and paints. That is a thought projected from the artist's brain, and its duration will be proportionate with its truth.'"

In explanation of why he chose to put out so much of the creative work of his brain under the signature of a woman, and how he happened to use the name Fiona Macleod, Sharp explained that when he began to realize how strong was the feminine element in the book Pharais, he decided to issue the book under a woman's name and Fiona Macleod "flashed ready-made" into his mind. "My truest self, the self who is below all other selves must find expression," he explained. The Self that is above the other self is what he should have said. The following extracts are from the Fiona Macleod phase of William Sharp and are characteristic of the Self, as evidenced in all instances of Illumination, particularly as these expressions refer to the nothingness of death, and the beauty and power of Love. "Do not speak of the spiritual life as 'another life'; there is no 'other life'; what we mean by that, is with us now. The great misconception of death is that it is the only door to another world." This testimony corroborates that of Whitman as well as of St. Paul, notwithstanding all the centuries that separate the two. St. Paul did not say that man will have a spiritual body, but that he has a spiritual body as well as a corporeal body.

After the experience of his illumination, William Sharp, writing as Fiona Macleod constantly testified to the ever-present reality of his spiritual life; a life far more real to him than the sense-conscious life although he alluded to it as his dream. In one place he says:

"Now truly, is dreamland no longer a phantasy of sleep, but a loveliness so great that, like deep music, there could be no words wherewith to measure it, but only the breathless unspoken speech of the soul upon whom has fallen the secret dews."

Of the impossibility of adequately explaining the mystery of Illumination and the sensations it inspires, he says, speaking through the Self of Fiona Macleod: "I write, not because I know a mystery, and would reveal it, but because I have known a mystery and am to-day as a child before it, and can neither reveal nor interpret it."

This is comparable with Whitman's "when I try to describe the best, I can not. My tongue is ineffectual on its pivots."

Another sentence from Fiona:

"There is a great serenity in the thought of death, when it is known to be the gate of Life."

Like all who have gained the Great Blessing, the revelation to the mind of that higher Self, that we are, William Sharp suffered keenly. The despair of the world was his, co-equal with the Joy of the Spirit. Indeed, his is at once the gift and the burden of the Illuminati.

Mrs. Mona Caird said of him: "He was almost encumbered by the infinity of his perceptions; by the thronging interests, intuitions, glimpses of wonders, beauties, and mysteries which made life for him a pageant and a splendor such as is only disclosed to the soul that has to bear the torment and revelations of genius."

The burden of the world's sorrow; the longings and aspirations of the soul that has glimpsed, or that has more fully cognized the realms of the Spirit which are its rightful home; are ever a part of the price of liberation. The illumined mind sees and hears and feels the vibrations that emanate from all who are travailing in the meshes of the sense-conscious life; but through all the sympathetic sorrow, there runs the thread of a divine assurance and certainty of profound joy—a bliss that passes comprehension or description.

Mrs. Sharp, in the final conclusion of the Memoirs says "to quote my husband's own words—ever below all the stress and failure, below all the triumph of his toil, lay the beauty of his dream."

In accordance with an oft-repeated request, these lines are inscribed on the Iona cross carved in lava, which marks the grave wherein is laid to rest the earthly form of William Sharp:

"Farewell to the known and exhausted,
 Welcome the unknown and illimitable."

And this:

"Love is more great than we conceive, and death is the keeper of unknown redemptions."

They are from his higher Self; from the illumined "Dominion of Dreams."

Chapter Fifteen - Methods of Attainment: The Way of Illumination

Oriental philosophies recognize four important methods of yoga.

Yoga is the word which signifies "uniting with God." From what has gone before in these pages, the reader will understand that unity with God means to us, the uncovering of the god-nature within or above, the human personality; it means the attainment and retainment in fullness of cosmic consciousness. We do not believe that any one retains full and complete realization of cosmic consciousness and remains in the physical body. The numerous instances to which we allude in former chapters, are at best, but temporary flights into that state, which is the goal of the soul's pilgrimage, and the only means of escape from the "ceaseless round of births and deaths" which so weighed upon the heart of Gautama.

The paths of yoga then, are the methods by which the mind, in the personal self, is made to perceive the reality of the higher Self, and its relation to the Supreme Intelligence—The Absolute.

The various methods or paths are pointed out, but no one, nor all of these paths guarantees illumination as a reward for diligence. That which is in the heart of the disciple is the key that unlocks the door.

These paths are called:
Karma Yoga; Raja Yoga; Gnani Yoga; Bhakti Yoga.

Karma Yoga is the path of cheerful submission to the conditions in which the disciple finds himself, believing that those conditions are his because of his needs, and in order that he may fulfill that which he has attracted to himself. The admonition "whatever thy hand finds to do that doest thou with all thy heart," sums up the lessons of the path of Karma Yoga. The urge to achieve: to do; to accomplish; to strive and attain, actuates those who have, whether with conscious intent, or because of a vague "inward urge," devoted their lives to taking an active part in the material or intellectual achievements of the race.

There are those who are blindly following (as far as their mental operations are concerned), the path of Karma Yoga; that is, they work without knowing why they work; they work because they are compelled to do so, as slaves of the law; these will work their way out of that necessity of fulfillment, in the course of time, even though they blindly follow the urge; but, if they could be made to work as masters of the conditions under which they labor, instead of as slaves to environment, they would find themselves at the end of that path. Karma Yoga would have been accomplished.

"Work as those work who are ambitious" but be not thou enslaved by the delusion of personal ambition—this is the password to liberation from Karma Yoga.

Raja Yoga is the way of the strongly individualized will. "Knowledge is power" is the hope which encourages the disciple on the path of Raja Yoga. He seeks to master the personal self by meditation, by concentration of will; by self discipline and sacrifice. When the ego gains complete control over the mental faculties, so that the mind may be directed as the individual will suggests, the student has mastered the path of Raja Yoga. If his mastery is complete, he finds himself regarding his body as the instrument of the Self, and the body and its functions are under the guidance of the ego; the mind is the lever with which this Self raises the consciousness from the lower to the higher vibrations. The student who has mastered Raja Yoga can induce the trance state; control his dreams as well as his waking thoughts; he may learn to practice magic in its higher aspects, but unless he is extremely careful this power will tempt him to use his knowledge for selfish or unworthy purposes.

Let the student of Raja Yoga bear in mind the one great and high purpose of his efforts, which should be: the realization of his spiritual nature, and the development of his individual self, so that it finally merges into the spiritual Self, thus gaining immortality "in the flesh."

Does this "flesh" mean the physical body? Not necessarily, because this that we see and name "the physical body" is not the real body, any more than the clothing that covers it, is the person, although frequently we recognize acquaintances by their clothing. Immortality in the flesh means cessation from further incarnations, the last and present personality including all others in consciousness, until we can say, "I, manifesting in the physical, as so-and-so, am now and forever immortal, remembering other manifestations which were not sufficiently complete, but which added to the sum of my consciousness until now I know myself a deathless being."

To those who seek the path of Raja Yoga, we recommend meditation upon Patanjali's Yoga Sutras, of which there are several translations, differing slightly as to interpretation. We have selected some of the most important, from the translations by Johnston. They are designed to make clear the difference between the self of personality, and the Self, or atman which manifests in personality:

"The personal self seeks to feast upon life, through a failure to perceive the distinction between the personal self and the spiritual man. All personal experience really exists for the sake of another: namely, the spiritual man. By perfectly concentrated meditation on experience for the sake of the Self, comes a knowledge of the spiritual man."

The wise person seeks experience in order that he may attain to the standard of the spiritual man; doing all things for the lessons that they teach; working "as those work who are ambitious," and yet having no personal ambition. Looking on all life, and at the self of personality and knowing the illusion of the self he is raising the personal self to the spiritual plane; but always he has the handicap of the desires of the lower self, the personal, which "seeks to feast on life," because it is born of the external, and its inherent appetites are for the satisfaction and pleasures of that physical self.

We do not say to look upon the body with its needs and its desires, as an enemy to be overcome; or that its allurements are dangerous although pleasurable. No. We say to the student, "control the desires of the body. Make them do the bidding of the Self, because it is only by so doing that you can gain the immortal heights of god-hood, looking down upon the fleeting dream of personality, with its so-called pleasures, as a bad nightmare compared to the joys that await the immortals."

Therefore, concentrate upon experience for the sake of the Self that you are, and learn the lesson of your experience, throwing aside the experience itself, as you would cast aside the skin of an orange from which the juice had been extracted. Don't fill the areas of your mortal mind with rubbish—with memories of "benefits forgot;" or loves unrequited; or friendships broken; or misspent hours; or unhallowed words and acts.

Cull from each day's experience all that helps to develop the spiritual man—all that will stand the test of immortality—kind words and deeds; principle maintained; a wrong forgiven; a service cheerfully extended; a tolerance and generosity for the mistakes of others as well as for your own. These seem small things to the personal self—the ambitious, the gloating, the sense-desiring self of the personality; we scarcely take them into account, but to the Self that is seeking immortality, these are the grains of wheat from the load of chaff; the diamond in the carbon; the wings upon which the spirit soars to realms of bliss.

Meditate upon this sutra.

"By perfectly concentrated meditation upon the heart, the interior being, comes the knowledge of consciousness."

The heart is the guide of the inner nature, as the head is of the outer. Love, the Most High God, is not born in the head, but in the heart. The heart travails in pain through sorrow and loss and compassion and pity and loneliness and aspiration and sensitiveness; and lo! there is born from this pain, the spiritual Self, which embraces the lesser consciousness, enfolding all your consciousness in the softness and bliss of pure, Seraphic Love—the heritage of your immortality.

Meditate long and wisely upon this sutra.

"Through perfectly concentrated meditation on the light in the head, come the visions of the Masters who have attained; or through the divining power of intuition he knows all things."

There is a point in the head, anatomically named "the pineal gland"; this is frequently alluded to as the seat of the soul, but the soul is not confined within the body, therefore, it is in the nature of a key between the sense-conscious self and the spiritually conscious Self; it is like a central receiving station, and may be "called up," and aroused to consciousness by meditation. Realizing and focusing the light of the spiritual nature upon this part of the head, opens up those unexplored areas of consciousness in which the masters dwell, and the student knows by intuition, which is a higher aspect of reason, many things which were heretofore incomprehensible to the merely sense-conscious man.

The spiritual Self is not a being unlike and wholly foreign to our concept of the perfect mortal-man; all the powers of discernment which we find in mortal consciousness are accentuated, intensified, refined; all grossness, all imperfections and embarrassments removed; pleasure sensitized to ecstasy; love glorified to worship. "Shapeliness, beauty, force, the temper of the diamond; these are the endowments of that body."

The spiritual body is shapely, strong, beautiful, imperishable, as the diamond, with all its brilliancy. No vapory, uncertain, or unreal being, but the Real, with the husk of sense-consciousness dropped off, and only the kernels of truth buried in the chaff of Experience, retained from the experiences of the personal self.

"When the spiritual man is perfectly disentangled from the psychic body, he attains to mastery over all things and to a knowledge of all."

The spiritual Self, the cosmic conscious Self, must not be confounded with the psychic body, which is formed from the emotions—passions; fears; hatreds; ambitions; resentments; envy; regrets. Know thyself as a being superior to all baser emotions, and the mastery over them is complete. They are not destroyed, but converted into love—the everlasting Source of Life.

"There should be complete overcoming of allurement or pride in the invitations of the different regions of life, lest attachment to things evil arise once more."

It is said that the disciples, seeking the paths of Yoga, reach three degrees or stages of development; first, those who are just entering the path; second, those who are in the realm of allurements, subject to temptations; third, those who have won the victory over the senses and the external life—maya; fourth, those who are firmly entrenched behind the bulwark of certainty; the spiritual being realized: cosmic consciousness attained and retained.

"By absence of all self indulgence at this point, also, the seeds of bondage of sorrow are destroyed, and pure spiritual being is attained."

Self-abnegation and self-sacrifice have ever been the way of spiritual development; but we are prone to misunderstand and mistake the true interpretation of this admonition; men shut themselves in monasteries and women become nuns and recluses as a penance, in order to purchase, as it were, absolution (at-one-ness with The Absolute, which knows not sin); this is not the point intended here. Spiritual consciousness can not be bought; the desires of the personal self may be sublimated into divine force and power, through recognizing the desires of the self as baubles which attract and fill the eye, until we fail to see the glories of that which awaits us.

"Thereafter, the whole personal being bends toward illumination, full of the spirit of Eternal Life."

Here again, we have assurance that the spiritually-conscious man, the "luminous body" is not a being apart from the self that we know our inner nature to be, but rather it is the inner Self even as we in our ignorance and our lack of initiation, know it, raised to a higher realm of consciousness; our desires refined, spiritualized, made pure, and our faculties strengthened and immortalized. We do not withdraw from experience but we draw from Experience the lesson—the hidden wisdom of the initiate.

Meditate upon these sutras.

"He who, after he has attained, is wholly free from self, is set in a cloud of holiness which is called Illumination. This is the true spiritual consciousness."

This aphorism is self-explanatory. He who attains illumination, and afterward lives and acts from the inner consciousness—the spiritual man, is free from the desires of the sense-conscious life, with its consequent disappointments; he sees everything from the spiritual, rather than the mental point of view, and understands the phrase "and behold, all was good."

"Thereon comes surcease from sorrow and the burden of toil."

The one who has attained cosmic consciousness, acting always from the Self, and not from personal desires, is set free from karma; he has fulfilled the cycle; he makes no more bondage for himself; he is free and is already immortal.

"When that condition of consciousness is reached, which is far-reaching, and not confined to the body, which is outside the body and not conditioned by it, then the veil which conceals the light is worn away."

The acquisition of spiritual consciousness, Illumination, endows the mortal mind also, with a degree of power sufficient to penetrate the veil of illusion—the maya; the disciple then sees for the first time, all things in their true light. The separation between the personal self, and the spiritual being that we are, is so fine as to be like a cob-web veil, and yet how few penetrate it. The suddenness with which this awakening (for it is like awakening from a dream of the senses), comes, startles and surprises us, and then we become astonished at the transparency of the bonds that bound us to the limitations of the mortal, when we might have soared to realms of light.

"By perfectly concentrated meditation on the correlation of the body with the ether, and by thinking of it as light as thistle-down, will come the power to traverse the ether."

The Zens say that the way of the gods is through the air and afterwards in the ether. This means that we must evolve from the physical to the psychic, and thence to the etheric or spiritual body. This is the way of the many. It is only the few who attain to perfect spiritual consciousness while manifesting in the physical, but these do not have to undergo "the second death" which is the dropping off of the psychic body, and assuming the spiritual body. They attain to immortality in the flesh, (i.e., in the present personality).

"Thereupon will come the manifestation of the atomic and other powers, which are the endowment of the body, together with its unassailable force."

The body here referred to, it must be borne in mind, is the etheric or spiritual body, which possesses the power to disintegrate matter; the power to annihilate time and space; so that he may look backward into remote antiquity and forward into boundless futurity; or as the commentator says, "he can touch the moon with the tip of his finger"; the power of levitation and limitless extension; the power of command; the power of creative will.

These are the endowments of the spiritual body with which the disciple is seeking to establish his identity—that he may overcome the second death and become immortal in consciousness, here and now.

Of this spiritual, or etheric body it is said, "Fire burns it not; water wets it not; the sword cleaves it not; dry winds parch it not. It is unassailable."

Meditate upon this sutra.

"For him who discerns between the mind and the spiritual man (the Self) there comes perfect fruition of the longing after the real being."

When the disciple has once grasped the fact that he is a soul, and possesses a mind and a physical covering, he has entered on the way of Illumination, and must inevitably reach the goal; then shall he find "perfect fruition of the longing" after the perfect Self, and its completement in union with the love that he craves. "Have you, in lonely darkness longed for companionship and consolation? You shall have angels and archangels for your friends and all the immortal hosts of the Dawn."

Such are the Yoga sutras, or aphorisms, as enunciated by Patanjali.

If the aspiring one were to give up a whole lifetime to their practice, gaining at last the consciousness of immortal life and love, what a small price to pay.

Raja Yoga with its methods and exercises, is the path of knowledge, through application; concentration; meditation.

The practice of Raja Yoga will lead the student to the path of Gnani Yoga; and to the realization that Bhakti Yoga, the way of love and service will be included, not as an arduous task; not as a study, or as a means to an end, but because of the love of it.

Gnani Yoga comes as complementary to practice of the sutras because knowledge applied for the purpose of spiritual attainment brings wisdom. Gnani Yoga, then, is the path of wisdom. The follower of Gnani Yoga seeks the occult or hidden wisdom, and always has before him the idea of whether this or that be of the Self, the atman, or of the self, the personal, gradually eliminating from his desires all that does not answer the test of its reality in spiritual consciousness; he welcomes experiences of all kinds, as so many lessons from which he extracts the fine grain of truth, and throws aside the husks; he accepts nothing blindly or in faith, but "proves all things holding fast to that which is good"; not that he lacks faith, but because the very nature of his inquiry is to discover the interior nature and its relation to God.

There are many in the world of to-day who feel the urge toward the path of Gnani Yoga, because of the conviction that is forcing itself upon every truly enlightened mind, that civilization with all its wonderful achievements, does not promise happiness, or solve the question of the soul's urge. In short, the educated, and the well conditioned, if he be a thinker, and not submerged in maya, lost in the personal self, inevitably finds himself searching for the real in all this labyrinth of mind creations and sea of emotions, and then as a rule, he seeks the path of Gnani Yoga, because his intellect must be satisfied, even though his heart calls. The mystic, the teacher, and the philosopher are following the path of Gnani; so is the true occultist, but many who deal in so-called occultism are employing knowledge only, entirely missing the higher quality—wisdom.

Bhakti Yoga, the path of self-surrender; the thorny way through the emotions; the "blood of the heart," is the short cut to Illumination, if such a thing could be. But there is no "short cut"; nor yet a long road.

Some one has said there are as many ways to God as there are souls. And yet, all persons who are on the upward climb, are demonstrating some one of these four paths, or a combination of the paths. It is, however, a significant fact that we do not hear anything of the great intellectual attainments of the three great masters—Krishna, Buddha and Jesus, but only of their great compassion; their wonderful love for mankind, and all living things.

St. Paul, who was probably an educated man, as he held a position of prominence among those in authority, previous to his conversion, laid particular stress upon the love-nature as the way of illumination.

And Jesus repeatedly said "Love is the fulfilling of the law." What is the law? The law of evolution and involution; of generation and regeneration; when the time should come, that Love was to reign on the planet earth as it does in the heavens above the earth, then should the kingdom of which he foretold "be at hand," and in conclusion of this to-be, Jesus promised that the law would be fulfilled when Love should come.

So Swami Vivekananda in his exposition of Vedanta declares:

"Love is higher than work, than yoga; than knowledge. Day and night think of God in the midst of all your activities. The daily necessary thoughts can all be thought through God. Eat to Him, drink to Him, sleep to Him, see Him in all. Let us open ourselves to the one Divine Actor, and let Him act and do nothing ourselves. Complete self-surrender is the only way. Put out self, lose it; forget it."

Let us substitute for the words "God," and "Him," the one word Love, and see what it is that we are told to do.

Love of doing good frees us from work, even though we labor from early dawn until the night falls; so, too, if we have some loved one for whom we strive, we can endure every hardship with equanimity, as far as our own comfort is concerned. Few human beings in the world to-day are so enmeshed in the personal self as to work merely for the gratification of selfish instincts. The hard-working man, whether laborer or banker, must have some one else for whom he struggles and strives; otherwise, he descends to a level below that of the brute.

This is the reason for the family; the lodge; the community; the nation; there must be some motive other than the preservation of the personal self, in order to develop the higher quality of love which embraces the world, until the spirit of a Christ takes possession of the human and he would gladly offer himself a sacrifice to the world, if by so doing he could eliminate all the pain from the world.

How natural it is to feel, when we see a loved one suffering, that we would gladly take upon ourselves that pain; the heart fills with love until it aches with the burden of it; this love enlarged, expanded and impersonal in its application is the same love with which we are told to love God, and to "do all for Him." Do all for love of all the other hearts in the Universe that feel as we feel when their loved ones suffer—that is the way to love God—it is the only way we know. We only know divine love through human love: human love is divine when it is unselfish and eternal—not fed upon carnality, but anchored in spiritual complement.

The story of Abou Ben Adhem ("may his tribe increase") tells us how we may know who loves the Lord. The angel wrote the names of those who loved the Lord most faithfully and fully, and coming to Abou Ben Adhem asked if he should write his name, and received the reply that he could not say whether he deeply loved the Lord, but he was quite certain that the angel could "write me as one who loves his fellow-men." And, lo! when the list was made and the names of all who loved the Lord recorded, Abou Ben Adhem's name headed the list.

The Vedanta philosophy teaches non-attachment and Vivekananda himself says: "To love any one personally is bondage. Love all alike then all desires fall off."

To love only the personal self of any one binds us to the sorrow of loss and of separation and disappointment; but to love any one spiritually is to establish a bond which can never be broken; which insures reunion, and defies time and space.

We can not love all alike, though we can love all humanity impersonally. All desires that have their root in the sense-conscious plane of expression, will fall off when the heart is anchored in spiritual love; but let it be understood that spiritual love is not opposed to human love; we do not grow into spiritual love by denying the human, but by plussing the human.

Spiritual consciousness is all that is good and pure and noble, and satisfying in the mortal and infinitely more. It is the love of personal self plus the Self—the atman.

Love is never unrequited. It is never wasted; never foolish. Love is its own self-justification; if it be real love, and not vanity, or self admiration, misnamed, give it freely, and don't ask for a return; don't ask whither it leads; only ask if it is real—if the love you feel is for the object of your love, or if it is for yourself—for you to possess and to minister to your pleasure; ask whether it is from the senses or from the heart.

The way of the Bhakti yoga, is the way of love and service, because service to our fellow beings, is the inevitable complement of love. Where we truly love, we gladly serve. It has been said: "The chela treads a hair-line." That is to say, the initiate must be prepared to meet defeat at every turn. Not defeat of his object of attainment, but the personal defeat that so many seek in the delusion that the world's ideal of success is the real success.

In conclusion we can only repeat what has been told and retold many times by all inspired ones, of whatever creed and race; namely, think and act always from the inner Self, cheerfully taking the consequences of your choice. Let not the opinions of the illusory world of the senses balk and thwart you. Let not the "worldly-wise" swerve you from your ideal and your faith in the final goal of your earthly pilgrimage—the attainment of spiritual consciousness in your present personality; this is the meaning of immortality in the flesh Doubt not this.

Make love your ideal; your guide; your final goal; look for the inner Self of all whom you meet. "Learn to look into the hearts of men," says the injunction in Light on the Path; dismiss from your mind all the accumulation of traditional concepts and prejudices that are not grounded in love, and above all falter not, nor doubt—no matter what seeming hardships you encounter in your earthly pilgrimage; they are but the Indian-clubs of your soul's gymnasium—Experience. "Meet with Triumph and Disaster, and treat these two impostors just the same."

Triumph and Disaster as seen with the eyes of sense-consciousness are both illusions; but don't for this reason cease your work. The phrase "you must work out your own salvation" is true. So also, you must be willing to do your part in working out the salvation of the world; salvation means simply the realization of the spiritual Being that you are—the attainment of that state of Illumination which guarantees immortality.

Experience teaches one important lesson: Our sense-conscious life is filled with symbolic language if we have the inner eye of discernment. An unescapable truth is symbolized in our daily life by the evidence that we get nothing for nothing. Everything has its price.

Immortality godhood, will not be handed to you on a silver salver; neither can any one withhold it from you, if you desire it above all things. And, altho' it has its price, yet you can not buy it. A seeming paradox, but the Initiate will see it all clearly enough when the time comes.

"He who would scale the Heights of Understanding
From whence the soul looks out forever free
Must falter not; nor fail; all truth demanding
Though he bear the cross and know Gethsemane."

* * * * *

The discouraged student says to himself: "If Truth demands such sorrow and sacrifice as this, I will not serve her. It is a false god that would so try his devotees."

Have you not said it?

The toll you pay is not to the Divine Self within, but to the "keepers of the threshold," that guard the entrance to the dwelling place of the Illuminati.

Earthly lodges and brotherhoods are symbols of the higher initiations.

There is a common mistake in the idea that the invisible states of consciousness are chaotic, or radically different from the visible.

"As below, so above, and as above so below" is an aphorism constantly held before the eyes of the would-be initiate. Each of whom, must interpret and know it for himself.

If the student finds the Raja Yoga sutras difficult of comprehension or of practice let him meditate upon the following mantrams:

I know myself to be above the false concepts which assail the personal self that I appear to be. I am united with the All-seeing All-knowing Consciousness.

I abide in the consciousness of the Indestructibility and Omniscience of Being. I rest secure and content in the integrity of Cosmic Law which shall lead my soul unto its own, guaranteeing immortal love.

I unite myself with that Power that makes for righteousness. Therefore nothing shall dismay or defeat me, because I am at-one with the limitless areas of spiritual consciousness.

My mind is the dynamic center through which my soul manifests the Love which illumines the world. Only good can come to the world through me.

Much that is called Mental Science, New Thought and Christian Science has for its aim and ideal, avoidance of all that does not make for personal well-being, and worldly success. Avoid this ideal; distrust this motive. Be ever willing to sacrifice the personal self to the Real Self, if need be. If the ideal is truly the desire for illumination, and not for self-gratification, the mind will soon learn to distinguish between the lesser and the greater. Have you longed for perfect, satisfying human love?

You shall have it plussed a thousand fold in immortal spiritual union with your god.

Summary

In the foregoing chapters we have set forth only a few of the facts and instances which the inquirer will find, if he but seek, of the reality of a supraconscious faculty, no less actual, than are the faculties of the sense-conscious human, which type forms the average of the race.

This faculty, or rather we should say these faculties—because they find expression in many ways, through avenues correlative to the physical senses—prove the existence of a realm of consciousness, far above the planes of the mortal or sense-conscious man, and transcending the region known as the astral and psychic areas of consciousness.

All who have reported their experiences in contacting this illimitable region unite in the essential points of experience, namely:

The experience is indescribable.

It confers an unshakable conviction of immortality.

It discloses the fact that we are now living in this supra-conscious realm; that it is not something which we acquire after death; it is not to be.

This realm is characterized by a beautiful, wonderful radiant iridescent light.

"O green fire of life, pulse of the world, O love."

It fills the heart with a great and all-embracing love, establishing a realization of the silent Brotherhood of the Cosmos, demolishing all barriers of race and color and class and condition.

Illumination is inclusive. It knows no separation.

It announces the fact that every person is right from his point of view.

"That nothing walks with aimless feet; that no one life shall be destroyed; or cast as rubbish on the void; when God hath made the pile complete."

That Life and Love and Joy unutterable are the reward of the seeker; and that there is no one and only path.

All systems; all creeds; all methods that are formulated and upheld by altruism are righteous, and that the Real is the spiritual—the external is a dream from which the world is awakening to the consciousness of the spiritual man—the atman—the Self that is ageless; birthless; deathless—divine. On all sides are evidences that the race is entering upon this new consciousness.

So many are weary with the strife and struggle and noise of the sense-conscious life.

The illusions of possessions which break in our hands as we grasp them; of empty titles of so-called "honor," builded upon prowess in war; the feverish race after wealth—cold as the marble palaces which it builds to shut in its worshippers—all these things are becoming skeleton-like and no longer deceive those who are even remotely discerning the new birth.

The new heraldry will have for its badge of royalty "Love and Service to my Fellow Beings," displacing the "Dieu et mon Droit" of the ancient ideal.

The Dawn is here. Are you awake?

Manufactured by Amazon.ca
Bolton, ON